Shadowed

Shadowed

Victor Burgin

>
Shadowed
Authors: Victor Burgin, Anthony Vidler

Shadowed has been produced to accompany an exhibition held at
the Architectural Association from 9 October to 17 November 2000.

AA Publications are initiated by the Chairman of the Architectural
Association, Mohsen Mostafavi.

AA Publications
Editor: Pamela Johnston
Editorial Assistants: Clare Barrett, Mark Rappolt

ISBN 1 902902 16 5

AA Publications
36 Bedford Square
London WC1B 3ES
www.aaschool.ac.uk/publications

Printed in Italy by Grafiche Milani
Designed by Lucy or Robert

>
Front cover: Love Stories #2, 1996
Back cover: Szerelmes Levelek [Love Letters], 1997

Once out of the house, the moment she reached the street,
the moment she began to walk, the walk absorbed her completely,
delivered her from wanting to be or do any more than the
immobility of the dream.

Marguerite Duras, *The Ravishing of Lol Stein*

Madeleine was at the far end of the Pont de Neuilly.
He allowed her to get well ahead. He even thought of going home.
But there was something intoxicating and disreputable in this pursuit
that obsessed him. He continued . . .

Pierre Boileau and Thomas Narcejac, *D'Entre les Morts*

The Panoramic Unconscious:
Victor Burgin and Spatial Modernism

Anthony Vidler

1 Victor Burgin, *In/Different Spaces: Place and Memory in Visual Culture,* Berkeley, University of California Press, 1996.

In an essay, later published as a chapter of *In/Different Spaces,*[1] Victor Burgin emphasized the specifically psychological character of modernist space. He cited the note left by Freud on his death bed – a laconic statement to the effect that, rather than following the dictates of a Kantian *a priori,* space would be a result of introjection or projection – which is to say, a product of the thinking and sensing subject as opposed to the universal and stable entity envisaged since the Enlightenment. What this also implied, as Burgin developed in a series of studies, was that there existed a spatial unconscious, susceptible to analysis and interpretation. And it is this spatial unconscious, in its various iterations in high and late modernism, that forms one of the objects of Burgin's recent visual and textual works.

Two works in particular stand out as exemplifying the 'unconscious' of modern urban space: the 'panoramas' of Dominique Perrault's Bibliothèque de France, whose four glass towers, reminiscent of the Corbusian Ville Voisin plan for Paris of 1925, were completed as the last stage of President Mitterand's *grands projets* (his attempt finally to remould Paris in the image of the modernist ideal), and of Mies van der Rohe's Barcelona Pavilion, erected and demolished in 1929 and recreated in more or less accurate facsimile in 1986. Burgin's panoramic works, far from simply 'representing' these two buildings – one a high modernist structure restored in its similacrum, the other a late modern similacrum of high modernism – work through carefully construed optical means to open up the buried problematics of modernist space as a whole. As panoramas, they take their place within the instrumental visual technologies of modernism itself; as manipulated panoramas, they analyse their chosen genre, exposing its internal dynamics and psychological faults; as forms of vision intersecting the constructed spaces of the two buildings, they cut directly against the implied and framed space of the original works to compose a new form of space that is neither late modern nor postmodern, but rather a hybrid that poses questions about the nature of contemporary 'virtual' space.

Modernist Panoramas

Panoramas and modernism have been inextricably linked from the start. From Robert Barker's first panoramic views of London in 1787, through the various French, German and American versions of panoramas and dioramas in the nineteenth century, to the modernist urban observatories of Patrick Geddes and Le Corbusier, the panoramic gaze was a characteristic of the modernist will to the omnipotent view, a view that, following Enlightenment principles of transparency and visual surveillance, opened up all 360 degrees of an observer's turning eye. What before had been framed in the strict geometries of the cone of vision stabilized in an Albertian frame, was now multiplied in the horizontal panorama made up of cones reduplicated to infinity. The technical developments of photographic representation after Daguerre – the invention of the continuous film and the possibility of a true panoptic image in 1871, the transposition of diorama into camera obscura – all added an air of technological sophistication that simply confirmed the modernist tenor of the genre.

Panoramas were, in this sense, the privileged instruments of modernist urban vision. London, Paris, Berlin, followed by capitals throughout the world, were successively opened up to the panoramic gaze, first traced on translucent canvas at huge scale, then domesticated (with the help of photography) through engravings, thence to be reduplicated in wallpaper and photographic prints. Such a view, that transformed the urban domain into a landscape subject to all the possibilities of picturesque and sublime aesthetics, worked to represent the new scale of the city to its inhabitants while also acting as a visual guide for the architect-planner. Take, for example, the celebrated panorama of Schinkel's Berlin, where each of his buildings stand out like so many urban markers, points of reference that triangulate the otherwise chaotic roofscape of the city – a guide and verification of order. Such order, when translated into the literal triangulations of Haussmann's Paris, or encircled by the equally literal 'panorama' of monuments and streets in the Ringstrasse of Vienna, was no longer to be confined within the picture-frame perspective of Renaissance idealism. The infinite circles of the panoramic were demanded in order to reduce the city to some form of comprehensibility. This gaze was to be itself monumentalized in the diorama, and more so in the modernist museums invented to educate the modern citizen in the formal and social structures of the metropolis.

In 1892 Patrick Geddes founded an 'Outlook Tower' for Edinburgh, from the top of which a panorama would display the complex morphology of the settlement and its relations to the surrounding countryside; then, as one descended from floor to floor, successive rooms would display the widening relationships between the city and the world. Transforming the observatory turret (that had already been transformed into a kind of giant camera obscura by its former owner) Geddes claimed a new didactic purpose for the panoramas: 'for all practical purposes,' he wrote, 'you are inside the bellows of a huge photographic apparatus'. A mirror projected onto the wall the aspect toward which it was turned, literalizing and focusing the more artificial versions of the panorama current earlier in the century. Later Geddes installed an 'episcope', designed by the French geographer Paul Reclus, which presented images in depth, so that the visitor could see 'through' the earth along any selected path to its opposite point. The city, as Manfredo Tafuri has noted, was now subjected to a gaze informed less by the cultural mandarinism of the nineteenth-century *flâneur* than by the technological utopianism of the social engineer.[2]

2 Manfredo Tafuri, '*Machine et mémoire*: The City in the Work of Le Corbusier', in *Le Corbusier: The Garland Essays,* ed. H. Allen Brooks, New York, 1987, pp. 203-18.

Avant-garde modernists were quick to follow this example, as is shown by Le Corbusier's penthouse for Charles de Bestegui of 1929–31. This double vision of post-Baudelairian poetics and rationalist planning took the form of a small oval cabin on the main (eighth-floor) terrace, from which an observer could view the entire panorama of Paris through a periscope, its lens raised above the level of the walls of the terrace. (Indeed the terrace itself, with its high walls, provided a vision of Paris as exemplified only by the tops of its high monuments.) Conceived as a giant camera obscura, the Bestegui apartment as a whole represented the existing city to the spectator in controlled fragments – monumentalized set-pieces – as if, through the periscope, one was viewing the city already transformed into a museum, ready for the installation of the new urban scale of the Ville Contemporaine or the Ville Voisin, with their transparent glass skyscrapers widely spaced through a parklike ground cleared of the traditional streets and impacted houses. At the Salon d'Automne of 1923 the Ville Contemporaine was even exhibited in the form of a wide panorama on a curved surface, a form also deployed to present the Plan Voisin at the International Exposition of 1937. In 1929 Le Corbusier was to expand this panoramic vision to the entirety of world history. His Musée Mondial was conceived as a spiralling transparent pyramid – a continuous version of the traditional panorama or diorama, presented not in frontal or circular form, but followed by the observer through an unending sequence of spirals: 'The diorama becomes more and more vast and more and more precise', wrote Le Corbusier.[3]

3 Le Corbusier, *L'Architecture Vivante,* summer 1929, p. 36.

Psycho-Panoramics

While the modernist city may have been construed and constructed under the sign of the panorama, the modernist vision continued, on the surface at least, to be interpreted through the lens of the Albertian frame. Lacan's mirror-stage, itself developed as a paradigm of modernist subject-construction, operates ostensibly as a reflective picture. Its image of the subject – distanced, reversed, scaled down – stands ever remote from an ego that calls for its interiorization, a vision that forms the initial rift in a self that, at the first instance of social experience, has to be defined on the basis of paranoia, of schizophrenia, of anxiety. Hence, it is through the frame of anxiety, as outlined nearly thirty years later, that the picture is interpreted – a picture that, for all intents and purposes, has the function of not revealing that which the subject desires. It stands at that point – the void – at which the subject is lost to view.

The panorama, however, apparently escapes this frame; it encompasses in the sweep of the moving gaze that which the static reflection of the mirror refuses; it captures what is hidden outside the boundaries of the picture, fixing what is momentarily lost to sight. Stretched horizontally, its top, bottom and sides seem boundless – like that painting by Caspar David Friedrich which caused Heinrich von Kleist to feel as if his eyelids were stripped bare: the *Monk by the Sea,* whose bleak horizon seems endless, whose framing is simply a cut or rift in the otherwise infinite dark space. But of course, the panorama, when constructed as a true panoptic, is an equally enframing vision, itself closed in the circle or semi-circle of its own horizon. This is what Bentham understood and put to such direct use as an instrument of surveillance: the panoptic is a closed and internally reflective system. Lacan himself, as he imaged the enclosure in which the Id was self-enclosed, used the image of the stadium, a scene of battle strewn with debris, an oval wall at the centre of which stood the Id's impregnable castle. In this sense, the panorama might be construed as a continuous picture, frames joined end-to-end in an unbroken circuit, hemming in the subject that at each move of the head, each turn of the eye, attempts to escape its own, unrevealing reflection.

The body, as well as the eye, is trapped in this movement of the gaze, for the panorama, in its circularity, imitates and captures the view of a body in rotation, a body that is itself captured by its fixed central position. As the photographer and collector of panoramic photographs Joachim Bonnemaison expressed it, the panorama is 'not a matter of an object in a frame, as in conventional photography; nor of a narrative sequence, as in cinema, but rather of something in the order of gesture. Indeed the rotation on its own axis is a total body-movement – it is a body-gesture which, in panoptics, is transmitted into an instantaneous visual memory. What may seem like a technological invention is in fact an extension of the body – motion and a way of rendering motion.'[4]

4 'La photographe panoramique dans la collection Bonnemaison, entretien avec Joachim Bonnemaison, par Régis Durand', in *Panoramas,* Arles, Actes Sud, 1989, p. 34.

Here it is that the panorama seems, spatially and psychologically, to counter what for modernism was a primary attribute of space – its potential reach to infinity and the transparency that allows for this extended vision. The aerial panoramas of Le Corbusier's cities all exhibit this character (one celebrated in his theoretical writing by the term *l'espace indicible*) which, in a blend of Nietzschean optimism and Acropolitan aesthetics, seems to have been tied to the sense of de-realization both he and Freud felt on attaining the heights of the Acropolis for the first time. For while the panorama ostensibly presents and represents the totality of the horizon, and thereby the subject's reach to infinity, the image remains enclosed within the circle described by the subject's own position point – panoptic, but panoptical at one and the same time.

In this context, the panoramic unconscious might be represented by that which escapes, not the frame of the picture, but the circle of the panorama itself. This might theoretically be captured by a continuous movement of the body/gaze as it turns, erupting in spiral after spiral; but this would be to simply repeat what has already been captured by the gaze, a simple unwinding or unravelling of the circle as if projected in three dimensions around a sphere. What is lost to view in the panorama, in effect, is hardly to be captured on the surface of a curvilinear perspective that itself imitates our own unrectified vision. Here the intersection of another optic, one that is not seen by the panorama, and one that does not itself see the panorama, would perhaps open up both frame and circle for analysis – which is, in brief, what Victor Burgin has accomplished in his panoramic work on Mies and Perrault.

Corbusian Occlusions

That Perrault's recently completed, but still not entirely functioning, Bibliothèque de France borrows heavily from the two-century-long tradition of 'ideal' French libraries is well known: from the vaulted antique stadium conceived by Etienne-Louis Boullée for the Bibliothèque Royale just before the Revolution comes the sense of a vast rectilinear centre; from Henri Labrouste's Bibliothèque Saint Geneviève and Bibliothèque Nationale comes the notion of the library as idyllic garden (conflated and reduced by Perrault in the all-pervasive but inaccessible central garden of the new library). But the architecture of the overall project is unabashedly neo-Corbusian, harking back to the diagrammatic towers sketched as types for the Ville Contemporaine or the Ville Voisin, a concept of transparency somewhat awkwardly conflated with the expressive impulse of late-eighteenth-century *architecture parlante,* as the four towers emulate in blunt geometry the form of open books. An open garden that constitutes a blocked centre; a transparency that itself is blocked to shield the books inside from the light; a sign language that no longer signifies: a building, then, that for all intents and purposes multiplies architectural contradictions.

It is on the upper terrace of this oxymoronic composition that Victor Burgin sets *Nietzsche's Paris* (1999–2000), as a sequence of panoramas filmed from four station points, each one at the midpoint of a side of the rectangle. In modernist terms such panoramas, following the Corbusian tradition, would demonstrate the viewer's command of ineffable space in four directions: the glass towers would ideally offer no interference to the sweeping gaze of the post-Nietzschean citizen of the verdant city. In effect, however, the first impression is of a terrible claustrophobia: the circling camera is occluded at every moment by objects – solid-seeming, reflective, glass walls; greenery imprisoned in steel boxes; space tied in by railroad tracks, river, and obtruding buildings. What once was a dream of 'crystals of glass' set in a sea of verdure as far as the eye could reach, is now a banal mechanical landscape of cooling stations, grills, vents and the blind storage walls of the book towers.

This claustrophobia is accentuated by the closed loops of the panoramic circles themselves and their own internal motion as they slowly move around the podium of the library from station point to station point in a deformed spiral dance that, with the fragmentary sounds of Handel punctuating the sequence, takes on the form of an uncanny rondo. Far from being the leap of the *Übermensch* into infinite space (that would be Le Corbusier's response to his passionate reading of *Thus Spake Zarathustra*), this dance is tied into a classical knot that never leaves the precinct of the library. It is the more unearthly, for being constructed from the frames of a panorama that is not in itself moving. What seems on the surface to be a simple sweep of the camera, is actually a movie fundamentally diverted from its original form, as Burgin transforms the filmed sequence into still images, removes all colour and then all people, thence to re-animate the images digitally to produce the panoramic 'movement'. The effect of this virtual movement, superimposed, so to speak, on still images, is to heighten the sense of an urban landscape reduced to its elemental characteristics: a diagram, in some way, of an architecture that has already diagrammed its diagrammatic prototype. Burgin here brings into relief the uncanny that lurks beneath the entire Corbusian project: the unexpected return of the classical into the modernist; the suppressed dream of the architect to remove all people from view, if not from the city; the silence, and above all the stillness (the smoke from the chimney stacks does not move) of the panoramic gaze.

Miesian Optics

The universal space into which Mies van der Rohe inserted his elemental planes, articulating vertically and horizontally the places in which bodies might find momentary rest, was ideally gridded – the Kantian *a priori* – but thereafter irrevocably disturbed by the intrusion of specificity; a specificity made the more absolute by its material qualities – pure transparency and absolute reflectivity, marbled authenticity, steel purity, chrome limpidity – and constructed spatially through two fundamental artifices. One of these, suggesting an infinity of space by-passing space, slipping along polished surfaces, unwilling to be restrained by corners, extended the spatial discourse of

De Stijl with rigour; the other, fashioning corners as if they represented the intersections of joints both universal and particular, attempted to find a resolution (impossible in material terms, but always present as an ideal) to the corner as defined by a column (an 'ɪ' or a '+') both inside and out, as at once a marking of the grid and a defining of the interior space. Where space was stopped, so to speak, was in the surfaces themselves: either in the tangibility of green marble acting as the ground for the twisting figure of a statue; or in the tableau, itself panoramically conceived of the horizontal view through transparency. Hence the mullions of the glass wall of the project for the Resor House, Jackson Hole, Wyoming (1938), acting as three vertical markers of a horizontal panorama of the Rocky Mountains, photomontaged as if it was the termination of the domestic space; or, inside, the wide perspective of the space frame of the project for the Convention Hall in Chicago, ending in the also wide, also panoramic, surface of the US flag. In all these iterations, Miesian space, too quickly dismissed as universal and therefore non-existent, emerges as a complicated dance of plane, surface, and horizontal panorama.

Burgin's panoramas cut through this rectilinear system with surgical care, curving the perspective, passing through solids and voids indifferently, to produce an entirely 'other' space – one that 'sees' (in a way not predicted by Mies) the apparently straight lines of infinite modernity as 'originally' curved. It is as if the raw images produced by the lens of the eye were reproduced prior to their mental correction, and the inner, a-geometrical and warped space of ocularity revealed as the unconscious foundation of the grid. Like the flattened sphere of the earth peeled open by a Mercator projection (or, in Burgin's own terms, like a moebius strip) Mies's grids now collapse into spatial conjunctions that have a more haptic than optic presence.

In this unravelling, the portal to Burgin's new and hybrid space is Georg Kolbe's statue *Dawn*. Originally this figure, as it twisted and turned on itself in the one fixed corner of the Barcelona Pavilion, acted as a kind of anchor for a space that was otherwise entirely slipping and mobile. Like some textbook example of a form-in-the-round taken from Adolf Hildebrand in order to demonstrate the clear opposition of figure and ground, this statue provided the only refuge from infinity, its only domestication, so to speak. In Burgin's panoramas its role as 'hyphen', or shifter, from one sequence to the other turns it into a twisting element, in an equally twisted space, that moves to join the fractured remnants of contiguous spaces. The eye sweeps in a quasi-baroque movement over the transparent surface of a distorted curve – a fold, one might say, in the continuity of what was once striated, but is now smoothed out.

The three station points that mark each of the panoramic sweeps, the first looking towards the statue, the second close up but looking away, the third 'inside' the pavilion, return in this way to the statue, as if it in itself were unravelling, being digitally peeled like an onion to reveal the inner body-space suppressed, or repressed, by the universal grid. Here Burgin, as in his analysis of Corbusian transparency, optically constructs a spatial unconscious that, incidentally, also reveals the fundamental difference between the two kinds of 'original' modernism. Where the panoramic unconscious of Le Corbusier/Perrault emerges as occlusion and block, that of Mies is displayed as entirely non-visual – haptic in Walter Benjamin's terms – and virtually blind. In a construct like the Barcelona Pavilion where, as Burgin remarks, there is 'no point of rest', the digitally reconstructed panorama gives us only infinite return. The zoom back towards the statue time and again dissolves into a loop that turns on itself, creating its own loop in architectural space – a topological figure of desire and non-fulfilment that matches the Lacanian moebius, a figure now flayed and its surface remastered into a single horizontal line that is joined to itself at each end. Rather like a line of code.

Virtual Analysis

In these movies that are not true movies, these panoramas that are not true panoramas, turned towards buildings that are not, as simulacra of their originals, true buildings, Burgin has succeeded in inventing a new kind of space that is not itself 'true' space. Or at least not true space in the way imagined by the modernists: therapeutic, open, transparent, infinite, *indicible*. Burgin's not-space is at once virtual (its moves are entirely digitally controlled and its effects digitally rendered) and analytical (it reveals what Freud posited were repressed – the motives of projection and introjection). This is not to say that it 'literalizes' the virtual, but rather that it utilizes the virtual in order to make manifest the models by which we might interpret the spatial unconscious, models that are, not coincidentally, spatial themselves. We have represented them as deformations of already known topologies – curved perspectives, moebius strips, grids and so on. In this sense we might consider Burgin's panoramics as kinds of diagrams, in the same way as Freud was to diagram the 'architectonics of the unconscious', or Lacan was to explore the topologies of desire. But where these were spatial models of primary unconscious domains and their structural relations (models made spatial in order to reveal and predict the intricate behaviour of the unconscious), Burgin's models are visual constructs that are aimed at analysing dimensions of the spatial unconscious.

Here the virtual becomes an instrument of analysis in its own right, rather than a simple re-representation of the already represented, a visual pun or trick of vision, or an iteration of what has not yet been envisaged. Digital camera movements zoom in and out, perspective is 'corrected', space is doubled on itself, looped and warped, stills are altered and animated, moving images translated into stills, like so many analytical procedures. If Freud's dilemma, as noted in the preface to the Wolf Man's analysis, was to combine a narrative of the analytical process with a restored narrative of the subject's unconscious life, and these with a structural account of the subject's condition, then Burgin has, with the aid of the virtual, brought together these three different dimensions in a single procedure. The first panoramic gives us a narrative vision of the subject, in the raw, so to speak; the second, transformed into stills, analyses the states of the subject at different spatial points; the third, and final, 'panorama' gives us both of these, together with the final, structural, results of the analysis. But where Freud's triple procedure would, in the spirit of science, leave us with a restored and healthy subject, whole once more, Burgin's leaves us with an entirely different space, a space *produced* out of analysis, and inconceivable without it. This space is neither 'modernist' nor 'postmodernist' in conventional terms. It at once surpasses the object of its analysis and is constructed out of it; it is a space that draws on the modes of representation defined by painting, photography, movies and video, but is none of them; it is a space that is, finally, not simply a product of some 'digital' imaginary. Rather this hybrid form, that we might call 'psycho-(pan)optics', is a space built up from the fragments that its procedures break out of the supposedly whole object. This is the object reduced to its pre-mirror-stage condition, re-formulated, not into its real unity, but into a post-mirror-stage topology that binds fractures and totalities into the interminable loops of analytical vision. Following the conclusions of Lacan's mirror-stage essay, we might say that where he brings us to the realization of the fundamentally paranoid and schizophrenic nature of the ego by claiming that analysis can go no further, Burgin's spatial models produce a paranoid architecture in the virtual form that is its only medium. And this would leave us with the discomforting conclusion that modernism and its later iterations, as architectures with a claim on our psyches, were, from the outset, a troubling case, the study of which has only just begun.

The Remembered Film

Victor Burgin

The first sequence:

A static view across a corner of a park. In the foreground a mound of freshly excavated earth alongside a path. In the background some high-rise buildings. In long shot a woman enters frame right. The camera dollies alongside as she walks along the path, then stops and pans to follow her as she turns to walk uphill and out of frame. Cut to a high point of view, looking downhill. In very long shot, diminutive in the cityscape, the woman climbs a path towards the camera. She arrives at an area set out with rows of benches. In the foreground a man sits reading a newspaper. The woman sits some rows behind him. Her head is framed in close-up against the sky. The wind tugs at her hair. She begins to cry. She cries as if the same undisclosed impulse that led her to walk now leads her to cry, as if her weeping continued her walking.

The second sequence:

A static view across a valley of fields and woods. In long shot a woman enters frame right, walking briskly and glancing back across the vale. The camera pans and tilts left to follow her as she crosses the frame. She turns to look uphill in the direction she is walking. Dissolve to a high point of view, looking downhill. In very long shot, diminutive in the landscape, the woman walks along a path towards the camera. Dissolve to a medium shot as she advances through a stand of trees. Clearing the grove she confronts a distant view of a cathedral seen above tree tops. Her head is framed in close-up against the sky. The wind tugs at her hair. She seems to hear music and voices in the wind. The sounds end abruptly on a cut to a very long shot of the woman alone and small in the landscape.

1 The original title of *Vive l'amour – Aiqing wansui* – literally means 'Love and Affection'. My thanks to Tatsuya Matsumura for telling me this.

The first sequence, of about twelve minutes' duration, is in colour and is from Tsai Ming-Liang's film *Vive l'amour*.[1] The second sequence, of about five minutes' duration, is in black and white and is from Michael Powell and Emeric Pressburger's film *A Canterbury Tale*. Fifty years separate the two films: the first is from 1994, the second from 1944. Some fifteen thousand miles separate their settings: Taipei, on the island of Taiwan, and Breeden Hill, near Canterbury in the South of England. Nevertheless, the two scenes have become inseparably associated in my memory. Both show a woman walking, but although I can recall other such scenes none of them cling together so insistently as do these two. If I replay them I can see relations of antithesis between them: town and country, old world and new, East and West. I can also see figures of antithesis within them: the urban park in Tsai Ming-Liang's film is a scene of devastation, a wasteland pitted with flooded craters and littered with uprooted stakes, spattered at the edges by red spots of flowers in tubs, suggesting the carnage of warfare in a place of peaceful recreation; the verdant idyll in Powell and Pressburger's film is studiously oblivious to the World War raging beyond its tranquil frame. Such observations after the fact might explain my tendency to think of the two sequences

together, but I feel there must be more than merely formal grounds for my association of the two. I know the stories told in the two films, I know what I am supposed to feel, and what judgements I might make, but the peculiarity of my relation to the sequences has nothing to do with the stories in which they were originally embedded. The narratives have dropped away, like those rockets that disintegrate in the atmosphere once they have placed their small payloads in orbit. Detached from their original settings each scene is now the satellite of the other. Each echoes the other, increasingly merges with the other, and I experience a kind of fascinated incomprehension before the hybrid object they have become.

In his book *Camera Lucida* Roland Barthes speaks of being emotionally touched by a detail in a photograph. The image is a family portrait made in Harlem in 1926 by James van der Zee. The people in the photograph, two women and a man, are unknown to Barthes. He nevertheless feels 'a kind of tenderness' aroused by the ankle-strap on the shoes worn by one of the women. At first he cannot account for the feeling, but later, remembering the picture, he realises that the emotion he felt was prompted not by the ankle-strap but by the woman's necklace. He now recalls a similar necklace

2 Roland Barthes, *Camera Lucida* (1980), New York, Hill and Wang, 1982, p. 53.

3 Sigmund Freud, 'Hysterical Phantasies and their Relation to Bisexuality' (1908), *The Standard Edition of the Complete Psychological Works of Sigmund Freud (SE)*, London, Hogarth Press and the Institute of Psycho-Analysis, 1974, vol. 9, p. 160.

once worn by an aunt who had passed all of her life by her mother's side in a dull provincial town. Barthes writes: 'I had always been saddened whenever I thought of her dreary life.'[2] No road of reason leads from the smart strapped shoe in Harlem to the sad life in a French town. The connection could not have been anticipated, and although it was involuntary it was not immediate. Barthes says the photograph 'worked within' him before he knew where the feeling came from. One of Freud's patients told him that she had once suddenly found herself in tears while walking in the street.[3] When she asked herself what she might be crying about she came up with a fantasy. She imagined she had had an affair with a well-known pianist, and had had a

child by him; she imagined that her lover had then deserted her and the child, leaving them in poverty. This fantasy, she believed, was the cause of her tears. Freud found that emotions, 'affects', may become dissociated from the 'representations', such as memory-traces or fantasy images, to which they were first attached.[4] The anecdote told by Freud's patient illustrates how an affect may be experienced in isolation from the representation with which it was originally associated. The account Barthes gives of his response to the family photograph shows how the affect may not only be detached from the original representation but displaced onto other representations. It illustrates how in the course of everyday life a chance encounter with an

4 See André Green, 'Conceptions of Affect', in *On Private Madness*, London, Hogarth, 1986.

5 We might more accurately say 'suppressed' as Barthes is himself able to recover the idea from the preconscious.

image may give rise to an inexplicable feeling, and how, by retracing the path taken by the affect, we may be led back to its origin in a suppressed or repressed idea.[5] Freud's patient identifies no equivalent of the image of the necklace to trigger the emotion she felt. But there must have been some precipitating cause, otherwise why did she burst into tears at that moment and not at some other?

We have probably all had the experience of finding that our mood has taken a turn for better or worse without our knowing why. It may take the prompting of someone close to us to lead us to uncover the cause in a memory or fantasy, perhaps provoked by a real or remembered image. Or we may find the cause without external help, by groping around in the dark. Before Barthes attributes his feeling of tenderness to the sight of the ankle-strap, he first mentions the belt on the woman's dress. Later, he reassigns the provoking cause of the emotion to the woman's necklace. On the trail of the enigmatic feeling he passes from a scene (the family group) to an object within the scene (the ankle-strap) to a gesture (the circling of a body part) that is first displaced throughout the scene (belt, shoe, necklace), and then beyond this scene to another scene (the life of the aunt). Barthes says the photograph 'worked within' him, as a silent and unselfconscious process. After Freud we may identify this process as that of the 'dream-work', the workings of the unconscious which are not confined to the dream but pervade our waking life. Barthes traces his feeling of tenderness to a memory. Freud's patient traces her tears to a fantasy. But it is unlikely that either of them had arrived at the end of the trail. For example, we may wonder why, in composing her fantasy of an ideal love affair, Freud's patient should invent such an unhappy ending. Who did the figure of the pianist represent that she should be so painfully punished for her relationship with him? As Freud provides no further details of this analysis we can only speculate.[6]

A model illustration of the mechanisms of associative chains is provided in an account of a case history given by the French psychoanalyst Serge Leclaire. Philippe, thirty years old, is in analysis with Leclaire. One day he goes for a walk in the forest with his niece, Anne. That night he dreams:

The deserted square of a small town, it is not quite right. I am looking for something. There appears, barefoot, Liliane, who I do not know, who says to me: 'It has been a long time since I have seen such fine sand.' We are in a forest and the trees appear curiously coloured, in bright and simple hues. I think that there are many animals in this forest, and, when I'm about to say this, a unicorn crosses our path. We walk, all three of us, towards a clearing we can see below.[7]

6 See Elizabeth Cowie, 'Fantasia', *m/f*, n. 9, 1984.

7 Serge Leclaire, *Psychanalyser: Un essai sur l'Ordre de l'Inconscient et la Pratique de la Lettre,* Paris, Seuil, 1968, p. 99, my translation. [*Psychoanalyzing: On the Order of the Unconscious and the Practice of the Letter,* Stanford, Stanford University, 1988, p. 70.]

Philippe's associations to the dream lead to three memories from childhood. He recalls a square at the centre of a small provincial town in France. In the square is a drinking fountain topped by a carving of a unicorn. This is the fountain that he felt was missing from the square in his dream. He remembers drinking at the fountain when he was three years old, cupping his hands to receive the water. During his walk with Anne the previous day Philippe had remarked on their surroundings. He said he had not seen such brightly coloured heather since a holiday in Switzerland when he was five years old. It had been on this holiday that he had learned from an older boy how to make the sound of a siren by cupping his palms and blowing between them. Philippe now remembers a holiday at the beach when he was about the same age. He was left in the care of his mother's cousin, Lili. He was always thirsty that summer and Lili affectionately mocked his repeated solicitations. The small Philippe would complain: 'I'm thirsty' *(J'ai soif)*; 'Me-I, I'm thirsty' *(Moi-je, j'ai soif)*. Lili names him after one such formulation, hailing him with the words: 'Philippe-I'm-thirsty' *(Philippe-j'ai-soif)*. This expression becomes the secret sign of their complicity. Philippe can now identify the 'unknown' woman in the dream, disengaging his childhood guardian 'Lili' and his companion of the day 'Anne' from the name 'Liliane' where they were entangled. Philippe's further associations eventually lead into normally inaccessible reaches of unconscious formations, into what Freud called the 'umbilical' of the dream. Leclaire's account of the dream of the unicorn, and a related dream, extends across several essays and a book. The analysis allows Leclaire to believe he has reached: '. . . an endpoint beyond which we cannot go: . . . one of those knots that constitute the unconscious in its singularity.'[8] This singularity, according to Leclaire, is composed of the elements he calls 'letters'.

The 'letter' is the imaginary representation of a corporeal site, the psychical representative of either an erotogenic zone or some other inscription on the body. In the case of Philippe such 'letters' include a scar (the place where a gaping of the corporeal envelope has been filled), the gesture of cupped hands, and the syllable *zhe (je)*. In the vicissitudes of a personal history such cuts, hollows and vibrations may become no less components of the corporeal imaginary than are the oral and anal apertures specified in 'classical' accounts of the component drives.[9] The 'letter' belongs to that

8 Serge Leclaire, *Psychoanalyzing: On the Order of the Unconscious and the Practice of the Letter,* Stanford, Stanford University, 1988, p. 83.

9 Freud himself was led, in considering hypochondria, to extend the concept of 'erotogenic zone' even to the internal organs. See, 'On Narcissism: An Introduction' (1914), *SE,* vol. 14, p. 84.

class of 'objects without otherness' of which Lacan says: 'They are the lining, the stuff or the imaginary thickness of the subject himself who identifies with them'.[10] After following the twists and turns of Philippe's associations – like so many converging, diverging and intersecting paths in a forest – what most interests Leclaire is the way in which all such imaginary derivatives of Philippe's primitive relation to the body, from which the maternal body has not yet been dissociated, have become condensed in the sounds of a secret name which the child gave to himself, 'Poordjeli'. Leclaire writes from within Lacan's circle and it is unsurprising that the 'letter' he emphasizes is one that may take a phonemic form. Nothing in Leclaire's account, however, commits us to such exclusivity. It is clear, for example, that the epidermal sensation of contact with a grain of sand is amongst the primitive 'letters' tallied in Philippe's analysis. Nevertheless, the secret name illustrates most clearly the mechanisms of the unconscious processes at issue here. The 'por' of 'Por-Je-Li' is formed from broken-off syllables of the subject's first and middle names: Phili-*pp*-e and Ge-*or*-ges, and is also contained within other key words in the anecdotal material, such as *peau* (skin) and *corps* (body). 'Je' also part of *Georges*, it is the *je* of *Moi-je,* of *j'ai soif,* and a part of *plage.* It is the *je* of his engulfing mother's *je t'ai!* (I've got you!), and also part of *rage* (rage) and *sage* (used of a child who is well behaved). It is the monumental inscription of the monogram 'J. E.' on his grandfather's suitcase, that he later learns to decipher. 'Li' is of course contained within both 'Philippe' and 'Lili'. It is the erotic crossroads where they are amorously joined. It is also part of *licorne,* the image in which Lili and the phallus are fabulously combined. (Philippe has a scar in the middle his forehead.) As Serge Leclaire and his collaborator Jean Laplanche elaborate, in a co-authored essay, on the case history of *Philippe-j'ai-soif,*[11] they return to that semantically dense phonic image – *zhe*. The sound is used in common by everyone who speaks French. At the same time it plays a part in the irreducibly private staging of Philippe's desire. Laplanche finds an analogy in '. . . those puzzle drawings in which a certain perceptual attitude suddenly makes Napoleon's hat appear in the branches of the tree that shades a family picnic.'[12] In a scene equally available to us all, that means the same to us all, there is an opening onto a destination towards which only one of us will be drawn.

Outside a clinical setting, the anecdotal details of Philippe's personal

10 In conversation with Anika Lemaire, quoted in Anika Lemaire, *Jacques Lacan,* London, RKP, 1977. The letter belongs to the register of the imaginary. It is in the nature of an image, whether the image in question be visual, or tactile, kinaesthetic, olfactory, auditory, phonemic or monemic. What is essential in the letter is that it is the primitive representative of loss, derivative of the auto-erotic satisfactions of primary narcissism. In a Lacanian perspective it represents the 'alienation of the instinct in the signifier'. It is what Leclaire and Laplanche elsewhere call the 'elementary signifier' of the unconscious, an object of what Freud called 'primal repression'.

11 Jean Laplanche and Serge Leclaire, 'The unconscious: A psychoanalytic study' (1960), *Yale French Studies,* n. 48, 1972.

12 ibid. p. 135.

13 'Observation shows that dreams are instigated by residues from the previous day – thought-cathexes which have not submitted to the general withdrawal of cathexis, but have retained in spite of it a certain amount of libidinal or other interest . . . In analysis we make the acquaintance of these 'day's residues' in the shape of latent dream-thoughts; and, both by reason of their nature and of the whole situation, we must regard them as preconscious ideas, as belonging to the system *Pcs.*' S. Freud, 'A Metapsychological Supplement to the Theory of Dreams' (1917 [1915]), *SE*, vol. 14, p. 224.

14 D. W. Winnicott, 'Transitional Objects and Transitional Phenomena', in *Playing and Reality*, Harmondsworth and New York, Penguin, 1982, p. 30.

15 D. W. Winnicott, 'The Location of Cultural Experience', in *Playing and Reality*, Harmondsworth and New York, Penguin, 1982, p. 112 ff.

life are of little interest to others. But the mechanisms by which his life returns to him in an image flux may help us understand the modes of our reception of the everyday environment of images. I use the expression 'everyday environment of images'. For the sake of brevity I might refer to this environment simply as the 'envelope'. Inhabitants of wealthy nations are enveloped by images. Suppose I get up one morning with a day of leisure before me. Over breakfast I read a newspaper, looking at the photographs printed on its pages and forming mental images of events described in its columns. Later, in the street, I am seduced or assailed by advertising images of all kinds, from posters in bus shelters to images that cover the sides of high-rise buildings. I may be on my way to an art museum to spend time with a certain painting. Or I might have chosen to search for a recording of some music, flipping through images on the covers of compact discs. Later, I spend time browsing the shelves in a bookstore. Back at home I watch the evening news before going out to see a film. After dinner I search the Internet for hotels for a trip I am planning, scrutinizing pictures of façades and rooms. Then I desultorily zap my way through disparate television channels before giving up in favour of bed and the novel I came across while book-shopping. I fall asleep with the landscape of the novel before my mind's eye. Freud spoke of the 'day's residues'[13] that contribute to the formation of dreams. But before sleep, at any time of day, I may find myself caught in an inchoate waking dream in which recollections of recent encounters with images combine with memories and fantasies. The place of such constructs is, in Donald Winnicott's words, 'in the area between external or shared reality and the true dream'.[14] For Winnicott, this is quite simply the *location of cultural experience*.[15] Today, what we share in common in cultural experience is increasingly derived from the image envelope. In the most usual sense an 'envelope' is that which contains and conceals a letter. Our daily individual experiences of the image envelope may secrete derivatives of 'letters' in the psychoanalytic sense which Serge Leclaire has given to the term. In bringing insights from psychoanalysis to our understanding of our relation to the image envelope, the question of what is private and what is public must be held in suspense. The question cannot be decided in advance of the analysis, but only retrospectively, at its conclusion.

The example that Roland Barthes gives of his experience of looking at and remembering the van der Zee photograph is one of several examples collected in his book *Camera Lucida*. Such details as the necklace in this photograph, which move him in a way that is strictly incommunicable, he calls the *punctum*. Of course the *punctum* is not the only occasion for an emotionally invested experience of a photograph. Barthes acknowledges that there are photographs that many people in common will find moving, and for reasons that may easily be explained. Here, says Barthes, the emotion derives from 'an average effect, almost from a certain training'. He calls this common ground of meaning the *studium*. Barthes had made a closely similar distinction in an earlier essay, where he distinguished between the 'obvious' and 'obtuse' meanings of some film stills.[16] We may bring much the same distinction to other images from the everyday environment. I switch on the television. Two men are in a tense exchange in a bar in the tropics. One has announced to the other his intention of marrying. The other disapproves. He thinks the woman is no good. The marrying man, who I recognize as Jack Lemmon, asks his friend, who I recognize as Robert Mitchum, to make one more trip to sea with him. Then they will sell their boat and split the proceeds. 'Keep the money', growls Mitchum, 'for a wedding present'. Cut to the boat dock at night. Lemmon is in a tense exchange with another man. Behind them is a painted backdrop of palms. A woman arrives to wave from the dock as the boat departs. The palms behind her are real. I recognize the woman as Rita Hayworth. I feel slightly tense, a little anxious for Jack Lemmon. Also a little bored. Apart from the boredom I am obviously feeling what I am supposed to feel. I turn off the television. I open the current issue of *The Cableguide*[17] and identify the title of the film as *Fire Down Below*.[18] I read:

Fire Down Below (1957). A shady woman (Rita Hayworth) comes between fishing-boat partners (Robert Mitchum, Jack Lemmon).

This brief synopsis of the narrative tells me nothing I did not already know. Within minutes of switching on the television it was clear that a woman had come between these men. It was clear that Robert Mitchum loved Rita Hayworth but could not accept her because of her morally compromised

16 Roland Barthes, 'The Third Meaning' (1970), in *Image-Music-Text*, New York, Hill and Wang, 1977.

17 *The Cableguide*, November 1999.

18 Dir. Robert Parrish, 1957.

28

past. It was clear that Rita Hayworth was a good woman fallen on hard times who was marrying Jack Lemmon because he was a nice man. It was clear that she really loved Robert Mitchum. It was clear that Jack Lemmon would get hurt. It was clear that things would turn out disastrously for all concerned. The fragment I saw was all that was required to retrieve this narrative from the archive of the 'already seen'.[19] But already, in memory, the obvious meaning of the film is giving way to obtuse meanings. The 'already seen' of the story hovers like an aura around the sequence of the farewell at the jetty, but already the narrative is fading. The jetty scene is itself decomposing into its component images: Jack Lemmon against a nocturnal painted backdrop, Rita Hayworth on a jetty in a *nuit américaine* of blue-filtered daylight. What was once a film in a movie theatre, then a fragment of broadcast television, is now a kernel of psychical representations, a fleeting association of discrete elements: a voice full of urgency; the passive indifference of painted palms; a woman waving across the unbridgeable gap that separates the real jetty where she stands from the studio set where a man pretends to leave. The more the film is distanced in memory, the more the binding effect of the narrative is loosened. The sequence breaks apart. The fragments go adrift and enter into new combinations, more or less transitory, in the eddies of memory: memories of other films, and memories of real events.

In 1977 sociologists at the University of Provence began a ten-year oral history research project in which they conducted more than four hundred recorded interviews with residents of the Marseille/Aix-en-Provence area. They asked each interviewee to describe her or his personal memories of the years 1930 to 1945. They found an almost universal tendency for personal history to be mixed with recollections of scenes from films and other media productions. 'I saw at the cinema' would become simply 'I saw'.[20] For example, a woman speaks of her experiences as a child amongst refugees making the hazardous journey from the North of France down to Marseille. She recalls the several occasions when the column of refugees in which she was travelling was strafed by German aircraft. In recounting these memories she invokes a scene from René Clément's film of 1952, *Jeux Interdits,* in which a small girl in a column of refugees survives an air attack in which her

19 An archive that in principle includes even films unseen. For example, amongst the one-liners in the 'F' section of *The Cableguide,* I also read: '*For Your Eyes Only* (1981) James Bond (Roger Moore) races Russians to a sunken spy ship'; and, '*Forever Young* (1992) A test pilot (Mel Gibson), frozen in the 30s, thaws out in the 90s'. I have not seen either of these two films, but I already know the story of each – that is to say I know the underlying story *(histoire)* that will vary only in the telling *(récit)*. 'James Bond races Russians to a sunken spy ship' is simply another variant alongside 'Captain Courageous races pirates to a buried treasure'. Similarly, the frozen Mel Gibson thawing out in the 90s is an updated variant of Rip Van Winkle.

20 Marie-Claude Taranger, 'Une mémoire de seconde main? Film, emprunt et référence dans le récit de vie', *Hors Cadre,* 9, 1991.

29

parents are killed. The woman's speech however shifts between the first and the third person in such a way that it is unclear whether she is speaking of herself or of the character in the film. The interviewer learns that the woman had in reality been separated from her parents on the occasion of such an attack and had been reunited with them only after many anxious days without news. As the interviewer comments, 'It is reasonable to think that the death of the parents in the film figured the possible death of her real mother . . .'[21] From the confusion of subject positions in the woman's speech we might suppose that the scene in the film in which the parents of the young heroine are killed, when they place their bodies between her and the German guns, has come to serve as a screen memory covering her repressed fantasy of the death of her own parents. A 'screen memory' is one which comes to mind in the place of, and in order to conceal, an associated but repressed memory.[22] Freud remarks that screen memories are marked by a vivid quality that distinguishes them from other recollections. It seems that the woman's memory of the film has similarly become fixed on this one brilliant scene of the attack from the air, as if it were the only scene from the film she remembered.

21 ibid. pp. 55-6.

22 In the most common type of screen memory discussed by Freud an early memory is concealed by the memory of a later event. It is possible for an earlier memory to screen a later one. Freud also remarks on a third type, 'in which the screen memory is connected with the impression that it screens not only by its content but also by contiguity in time: these are contemporary or contiguous screen memories'. [Sigmund Freud, The Psychopathology of Everyday Life (1901), SE, vol. 6, p. 44.]

For me, it is as if the two scenes with which I began are the only scenes I have remembered from those two films. I know there are others, but it is as if they lack illumination. As I revisit them again in memory I find myself recalling the house in which I spent most of my early life. The house is on the side of a hill. When my mother went out shopping, or to visit relatives, or for whatever other reason, she would descend this hill. Before I was old enough to be left alone I would descend with her, and climb the hill afterwards. So much walking, so much climbing, clearly invested with great purpose by my mother, but so often incomprehensible to me. The house was in a fringe of houses bordering the tangle of streets and factories that filled the valley below. Beyond this fringe the paved streets gave way to dirt paths through ruined allotment gardens. The broadest path first ran alongside an industrial spoil heap. Then further paths turned off to lead higher, to the few remaining fields of a failing family farm, a part of the rural past stranded on these slopes as industrialization engulfed the valley. Beyond the farm the slopes inclined even more steeply and the trails struggled to a barren summit, where the wind tugged at the hair. As I try to bring my attention back to the fragments of film, I find another scene from childhood joining them. I now confront a mutating 'scene' in every sense that the dictionary allows this word: a view or prospect seen by a viewer; the place where an action or event occurs; the setting of a play, movie, novel, or other narrative; a subdivision of an act in a dramatic presentation, in which the setting is fixed and the time continuous; a shot or series of shots in a movie constituting a unit of continuous related action; the scenery and properties for a dramatic presentation; a theatre stage; a real or fictitious episode, especially when described; and a public display of passion or temper.[23] The memory that has joined the previous fragments is this:

23 From the *American Heritage Dictionary*.

The living room of a modest house. A small boy, perhaps four years old, is in the company of two women: his mother and her sister-in-law. They are standing together in front of a fireplace, above which is a mirror. The boy's aunt is trying on a blouse. The boy watches the women as they appraise the garment reflected in the mirror. The aunt removes the blouse, revealing a white bra. The boy is puzzled by the forms revealed, so different from those of his own flat chest. Trying on a word only recently acquired, he asks: 'Are those your tits?' The calm shatters. His aunt, pulling on her blouse, smiles but seems disconcerted. His mother is angry and makes reproaches he does not fully understand.

Could this be the originating occasion of my 'fascinated incomprehension' before the memory of the two film sequences, the matrix for my puzzling over what is the same and what is different between them? When I began writing this paper I had misgivings about making public my chance associations to two short sequences of remembered films. When the type of theoretical work on photography and film in which I have been involved emerged in the 1970s it was concerned with explaining the ways in which films and photographs contribute to the formation, perpetuation and dissemination of dominant systems of commonly held beliefs and values. It was emphatically not concerned with whatever irreducibly subjective meanings an image might have for this or that individual. It seems I need not have

worried. What I find at the end of my 'autobiographical' trail, which I supposed might concern no one but myself, is the *mise-en-scène* of a riddle we
all must answer at one time or another, in one way or another, and to which
we must perhaps find new answers each day of our lives: the enigma of
sexual difference. It is perhaps disappointing that the path I have followed
should have led only to such a banal fact as that of the difference between
the sexes. Narcissism prefers we arrive at more important or wonderful desti-
nations. But nothing is more important to the identity of the emerging
subject than this; the baffling fact of sexual difference presents the child
with an object of wonder. Certainly, the echoes of the questions that sexual
difference occasions, and of the 'answers' that lead only to more questions,
may be discerned throughout the popular productions of the media, and
those less popular productions we call 'art'.

The third sequence:
A static view down a wooded slope towards a large country house. Dissolve
to a long shot of a woman looking across a wooded park. Cut to a close-up of
a ripe fruit hanging from a branch. Dissolve to a solid red frame as a
woman's voice speaks some sentences in German. Cut to a medium shot of a
woman looking from a window towards a path winding up a meadow between
trees. Cut to a long shot of the woman on the path looking back towards the
house. Cut to a low point of view as the woman climbs the hill, nearing a
stand of trees at the summit. Cut to the woman seen from behind as she
looks over meadow and trees to the house below and the horizon beyond.

This third sequence is of about three minutes' duration and comes from my
own video projection work *Lichtung*. The work was shot in the Ettersberg
forest, near Weimar, and was first shown in 1999. The correspondences
between this sequence and others I have discussed here may be apparent,
but they did not occur to me until I had completed the penultimate draft of
this paper. The connections illustrate the observation with which I shall con-
clude. Chains of associations may lead as far into individual history as those
traced by Leclaire in his analysis of Philippe. More usually they lead no
further than Barthes travelled in his account of the van der Zee photograph,

or than I was able to go in my memory of childhood.[24] But associations lead not only to roots in personal history. In selectively incorporating fragments from the image environment they also branch out to weave private and public into a unitary network of meanings. In the end, the question, 'What is the origin of this psychical object?' is of less importance in life and theory than the question, 'What use am I able to make of the object?'[25] Our forgotten answers to distant questions may reverberate down history to shatter remembered films. But what concerns us most is what we make from the fragments.

24 Freud writes: 'It may indeed be questioned whether we have any memories at all *from* our childhood: memories *relating* to our childhood may be all that we possess. Our childhood memories show us our earliest years not as they were but as they appeared at the later periods when the memories were aroused. In these periods of arousal, the childhood memories did not, as people are accustomed to say, *emerge;* they were *formed* at that time. And a number of motives, with no concern for historical accuracy, had a part in forming them, as well as in the selection of the memories themselves.' [Sigmund Freud, 'Screen Memories' (1899), *SE,* vol. 3, p. 322.]

25 See D.W. Winnicott, 'The Use of an Object and Relating through Identifications', in *Playing and Reality,* Harmondsworth and New York, Penguin, 1982, p. 101 ff.

Remembering, Repeating

1995

A work for the inaugural exhibition of the newly constructed Museum of Contemporary Art in Lyon. That summer in Lyon and Paris there were bombs in the metro. Islamic groups claimed responsibility. French colonial history is inscribed in the mix of people who pass underground on the *tapis roulant* at Montparnasse metro station. Trains pass at night on an overground section of line. A woman running. Jean Gabin, in *Pépé le Moko,* running through the Casbah after the woman he loves. He falls. As he falls a woman in purdah rises.

Remembering, Repeating

Two-screen video projection, 1995
Two DVDs – 3-minute programme loops – colour – NTSC – stereo

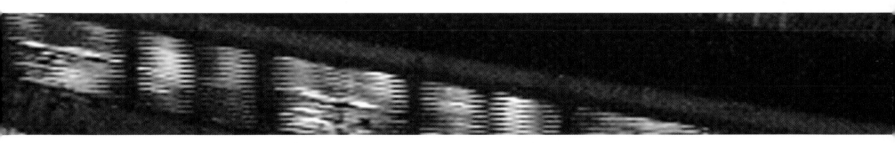

Love Stories # 2

1996

Invited to contribute a work to a small group show at a gallery in London, but with no time to go there, I used material shot closer to home in San Francisco and Las Vegas. Four basic building blocks: written words, video sequences, colour screens, fragments from film sound-tracks. On the wall, the sentence driving fast on empty freeways. In front of the wall, three plinths, each with a video monitor. On the screen of each monitor a short video sequence alternates with a screen filled with a solid colour. Each video sequence is shot in a public place. Nothing has been staged. The sequence plays in slow motion and there is no sound. The colour screen is accompanied by a fragment of sound-track from a classic Hollywood movie.

The disks are not synchronized, which allows chance relations between the images on the three monitors. By chance, the two women may appear to turn towards each other. Or all three colour screens may be displayed at the same time, so that all three voices sound simultaneously. At other times only a single voice is heard, accompanying whatever image the viewer may be watching. Each of the three sound-track fragments expresses a typical form of love relationship: a woman is attracted to a man because he reminds her of her father; a man is attracted to a woman because she reminds him of someone else; a woman despairs at her inability to match the perfection of her own ideal. In print their words are as banal as the synopsis of an opera. The meaning is in the grain of the voice.

Love Stories # 2

Three video monitors, plinths, wall text, 1996
Three DVDs – 3-minute programme loops – colour – NTSC – stereo

DRIVING

FAST ON EMPTY FREEWAYS

DRIVING

FAST ON EMPTY FREEWAYS

DRIVING

FAST ON EMPTY FREEWAYS

DRIVING

FAST ON EMPTY FREEWAYS

DRIVING

John Stahl
Leave Her to Heaven
soundtrack fragment, Gene Tierny

FAST ON EMPTY FREEWAYS

DRIVING

Alfred Hitchcock
Vertigo
soundtrack fragment, Kim Novak

FAST ON EMPTY FREEWAYS

Albert Lewin
Pandora and the Flying Dutchman
soundtrack fragment, Ava Gardner

DRIVING

FAST ON EMPTY FREEWAYS

Szerelmes Levelek [Love Letters]

1997

A work for the Mücsarnok Museum, Budapest. Psychoanalysis flourished in Hungary until Fascists killed or scattered its practitioners. Under the post-war communist regime the practice of psychoanalysis was forbidden. Even today there are few works in Hungarian by Sándor Ferenczi, one of the earliest and most brilliant of Freud's collaborators. In 1900, eight years before he first met Freud, Ferenczi had begun an illicit love affair with Gizella Pálos, a married woman eight years his senior. Gizella had two daughters. Her younger daughter, Magda, had married Ferenczi's younger brother, Lajos. But her elder daughter, Elma, seemed incapable of forming any lasting relationship. Gizella was concerned about this. At her request, in the summer of 1911, Ferenczi took Elma into analysis. Elma was then twenty-four years old, Ferenczi was thirty-eight. In December 1911 Ferenczi wrote to Freud to confess that he and Elma had fallen in love.

Gizella placed her daughter's happiness above her own. In spite of her own distress she gave her blessing to Elma's marriage to Ferenczi. But Gizella's husband, Géza Pálos, voiced mild objections. Elma's indecisive response to her father's reservations unpleasantly surprised Ferenczi. As he expressed it, 'at this moment, she showed not the pure joy of a lover but rather the pain of her emotional wounds'.[1] He wrote to Freud: 'The scales fell from my eyes . . . I had to recognize that the issue here should be one not of marriage but of the treatment of an illness.'[2] Ferenczi suspected that what Elma felt for him was a displacement of her love for her father. He postponed further talk of marriage until analysis could determine who Elma 'really' loved. Freud reluctantly agreed to take over Elma's psychotherapy but treated her for only three months. Ferenczi then vacillated between Elma and Gizella as he questioned whether Elma's love for him was anything other than 'father transference'. Freud confirmed Ferenczi's doubts and strongly advised him against marrying the younger woman. Elma eventually went to America where she married a journalist. At the news of her marriage Ferenczi fell ill. In 1919, while recovering from his illness, he proposed to Gizella, now divorced. On the morning of the wedding, Elma's father died of a heart attack. Sándor Ferenczi and Gizella Pálos remained married until Ferenczi's death, but Ferenczi never concealed from his wife that his passion for her daughter was undiminished. In 1921, in a letter to Georg Groddeck, he bitterly blamed Freud for having encouraged him to drive into exile the woman he loved most.

1 Eva Brabant, Ernst Falzeder, Patrizia Giampieri-Deutsch (eds.), *The Correspondence of Sigmund Freud and Sándor Ferenczi*, Volume 1, 1908-1914, Cambridge, Massachusetts, and London, Harvard, 1993, p. 326.

2 ibid. p. 324.

71

Ferenczi coined the expression 'father transference' to speak of Elma's feelings for him. The idea of 'transference' emerged at the very beginning of psychoanalytic theory. But it was easily subsumed under the more general concept of 'displacement', and its specificity was not brought into focus until the publication of Freud's paper 'Observations on Transference-love'. Freud's essay was published in 1915, four years after Ferenczi had confessed his love for Elma. Ferenczi had written to Freud: 'I was not able to maintain the cool detachment of the analyst with regard to Elma.'[3] In his essay, Freud observes: '[it is] not always easy for the doctor to keep within the limits prescribed by ethics and technique. Those who are still youngish . . . may in particular find it a hard task.'[4] In 1915 Freud was on the eve of his sixtieth birthday. Ferenczi had not long turned forty. From Freud's vantage point his Hungarian colleague must have appeared 'still youngish'. There can be little doubt that when Freud wrote his paper on transference-love the relationship of Elma Pálos and Sándor Ferenczi must have been prominent amongst his thoughts.[5]

In my work for the Mücsarnok I restored these two previously disparate items – Freud's 'dispassionate' observations on psychoanalytic technique, Ferenczi's conflict of emotions and ethical principles – to their original proximity. The installation took the form of three large projected video images in three galleries (iv, v and vi) that connect in a straight line, like the compartments of a railway carriage. There was much coming and going between Budapest and Vienna in the course of the Ferenczi/Gizella/Elma affair. What is seen in the video consists mainly of images of the Hungarian landscape shot from the train between Budapest and Vienna. The images are identical in each room, but the sound heard with the images changes as the viewer passes from one room to the next. The sound heard in gallery iv is of a voice telling the story of the triangle Ferenczi/Gizella/Elma from Ferenczi's point of view. The text is based on edited excerpts from his letters to Freud. The sound heard in gallery vi is of a voice speaking a précis of Freud's essay on transference-love. In room v these previously separated monologues come together in a dialogue. In allusion to the otherwise 'silent' figures of Gizella and Elma the words of Freud are spoken by a mature woman, and those of Ferenczi by a young woman. The first sentence on the sound-track is adapted from Ferenczi's letter to Freud dated July 22, 1909. The final sentence is from his letter of November 18, 1917. The intervening period occupies 739 pages

3 ibid. p. 318.

4 Sigmund Freud, 'Observations on Transference-love' (1915 [1914]), *The Standard Edition of the Complete Psychological Works of Sigmund Freud (SE),* London, Hogarth Press and the Institute of Psycho-Analysis, 1974, vol. 12, pp. 157-71.

5 Thoughts which would also have included the Carl Jung/Sabina Spielrein affair. See Lisa Appignanesi and John Forrester, 'Sabina Spielrein and Loë Kann: Two Analytic Triangles', in *Freud's Women,* New York, Basic, 1992.

of the published correspondence between Freud and Ferenczi, but takes only a page and a half of my 'script'. In the interests of narrative continuity I have shuffled some written fragments out of their actual historical order, though the sequence of the events they describe is maintained. Freud's paper on transference-love occupies seven pages of the *Standard Edition* of his work. It, too, is condensed into a page and a half of sound-track script.

In his 1921 book *Group Psychology and the Analysis of the Ego* Freud notes that the element of idealization of the object, commonly found in the erotic love of one individual for another, is fundamentally similar to that found in the devotion of the group to the leader (and/or to the idea – or 'cause' – that the leader represents). As a consequence, 'everything that the object does and asks for is right and blameless . . . in the blindness of love remorselessness is carried to the pitch of crime.'[6] Sándor Ferenczi died in 1933, the year Adolf Hitler was appointed Germany's Chancellor. After the German annexation of Austria in March 1938, the Princess Marie Bonaparte travelled to Vienna to add her own voice to those trying to persuade Freud to leave. As on previous occasions, she took along a small movie camera to record her visit to the Freud household. On this trip, exceptionally, she took her camera into the street. She titled the resulting short sequence *Le 1er Mai à Vienne après l'Anschluss*. On this day Hitler paraded through Vienna to receive the adulation of the crowd. The parade itself is not seen in Marie Bonaparte's film. Her camera pans across the façade of Berggasse 19, the building where Freud had lived and practised for forty-seven years, now draped with swastika banners. It frames the massed crowds cheering Hitler. All the shots are taken at a distance from, or from behind, their subjects. Except for one. At the very end of the sequence the camera momentarily dwells in full frontal close-up on the isolated figure of a well-dressed young woman. For about four seconds she hesitates, surprised before the camera. Then she is gone. This image appears in my video digitally reworked into longer sequences, and punctuates the images shot from the train.

6 Sigmund Freud, *Group Psychology and the Analysis of the Ego* (1921), *SE*, vol. 18, p. 113.

Szerelmes Levelek [Love Letters]

Three-screen video projection, 1997
DVD – 10-minute programme loops – colour – NTSC – stereo

Richard Strauss
Der Rosenkavalier
Act III (fragment), Elisabeth Schwarzkopf

Nem élek olyan magányban mint gondolná. Személyes jólétem addig tart, míg Frau Isolde társaságában lehetek – néha így szólítom Frau G.-t, mióta egy álmomban ezen a néven jelent meg. Kapcsolatunkban a teljes nyíltság elérésének nehéz és fájdalmas művelete gyorsan halad. Frau Isolde intelligenciája és az analízis iránt tanúsított érdeklődése eléggé erősnek bizonyult a leküzdendő ellenállás és a leplezetlen valóság elfogadásának keserűségével szemben.

I am not as alone as you might think. My personal well-being is good as long as it is possible for me to keep company with Frau Isolde – as I sometimes call Frau G., because it was her name in one of my dreams. The difficult and painful operation of producing complete candour in my relationship with Frau Isolde is proceeding rapidly. Her intelligence and her interest in analysis proved strong enough for the resistances to be overcome and the bitterness of the unvarnished truth to be accepted.

Frau Isolde iránti
érzelmeimmel kapcsolatban
be kell vallanom, hogy a
szerelmi vallomás amit
tettem, a fölény amellyel
némi vonakodás után, de
helyesen felismerte a
helyzetet, és az őszinteség
amely közöttünk lehetővé
vált, számomra még valós-
zínűtlenebbé tette, hogy
bármely más nőhöz láncoljam
magam, annak ellenére, hogy
Frau Isolde és magam előtt is
be kellett látnom más nők
iránt érzett szexuális vonzal-
mamat, sőt még
szemrehányást is tettem neki
idős kora miatt. Nyilvánvaló,
hogy túl sok mindent várok
tőle: szeretőt, barátot, anyát
és tudományos szempontból

As far as my feelings towards
Frau Isolde are concerned, I
must say that the confession
that I made to her, the superi-
ority with which, after some
reluctance, she correctly
grasped the situation, and the
honesty which is possible
between us, makes it seem
less possible for me to tie
myself to any other woman,
even though I admitted to her
and to myself having sexual
desires toward other women,
and even reproached her for
her age. Evidently I have too
much in her: lover, friend,
mother, and, in scientific
matters, an extremely intelli-
gent and enthusiastic pupil,
who completely grasps the
extent of the new knowledge.

egy kivételesen intelligens és
lelkes tanítványt, aki azok
teljességében képes felfogni
az új tudomány lehetőségeit.

Az egyik legnehezebb helyzet, amelyben egy pszichoanalitikus találhatja magát, az amelyben egy női betege kimutatja vagy nyíltan bevallja, hogy beleszeretett. A laikus számára a szerelemmel kapcsolatos dolgok összemérhetetlenek minden mással, külön oldalra íródnak, ahol más írás nem tűrhető meg. A pszichoanalitikusnak más szemszögből kell a dolgokat néznie.

One of the most difficult situations with which a psychoanalyst must deal is the one in which a woman patient either indicates, or openly declares, that she has fallen in love with him. To the

layman, things that have to do with love are incommensurable with everything else; they are, as it were, written on a special page on which no other writing is tolerated. A psychoanalyst must look at things from a different point of view.

Zavartan tapasztalom, hogy Frau G. nyilvánvaló libidó csökkenése bennem fejti ki hatását. Lánya, Elma, jelenleg kezeltjeim közé tartozik. Sokszor azon találom magam, hogy arról fantáziálok, feleségül veszem Elmát, és komolyan hiszem, Frau G. iránti hűségem csak szánalom. Ugyanakkor, Frau G.-vel folytatott mai beszélgetés - amelyet az én könnyeim kísértek - rádöbbentett, mennyire túlbecsültem képességeimet, amikor azt hittem, föl tudom oldani fixációm erős kötéseit.

I am disturbed to observe that an apparent detachment of libido from Frau G. is playing itself out in me. Her daughter Elma is now in treatment with me. I find myself having fantasies

about marrying Elma, and thinking seriously that I am true to Frau G. only out of piety. A talk with Frau G. today however, with tears on my part, showed me that I overestimated myself enormously when I considered myself capable of loosening the strong bonds of my fixation upon her.

*Amikor egy beteg beleszeret
orvosába, csak kétféle
kimenetel tűnik lehetségesnek.
Az egyik, ami ritkán történik
meg, hogy a körülmények
megengedik kettejük törvényes
tartós kapcsolatát. A másik
gyakoribb esetben orvos és
beteg elválnak, felhagynak
közösen megkezdett
munkájukkal. Persze
elképzelhető egy harmadik
lehetőség is, miszerint
törvénytelen kapcsolatba
lépnek, amely nem hivatott
örökké tartani. De ez mind a
társadalmi, mind a szakmai
erkölcsi normákat sértené.*

*When a patient falls in love
with her doctor it might seem
that only two outcomes are
possible. One, which happens
rarely, is that circumstances
permit a permanent legal
union between them. The
other, which is more frequent,
is that the doctor and patient
part and give up the work they
have begun together. Of
course a third outcome is con-
ceivable: that they enter into
an illicit love relationship that
is not intended to last forever.
But this would offend both
conventional morality and
professional standards.*

Be kell vallanom, nem voltam
képes megtartani az analitikus hűvös kívülállóságát
Frau G. leányával szemben.
Nem tudok továbbra is úgy
tenni, mintha az, amit Elma
iránti érzek, egyszerűen a
pszichiáter vagy az atyai
barát jóindulata lenne. Frau
G. mindenről tud, és egysz-
erre teszi könnyebbé és
nehezebbé helyzetemet páratlanul kedves és szerető
hozzáállása.

I am compelled to confess to
you that I have not been able
to maintain the cool detachment of the analyst with
regard to Frau G.'s daughter.
I can no longer pretend that
what I feel for Elma is simply
the benevolence of the
physician or of a fatherly
friend. Frau G. has been told
everything, and my situation
is made both easier and more
difficult by her incomparably
kind and loving attitude
toward me.

*Az analitikusnak elsőként azt
kell felismernie, hogy a beteg
szerelme az analízis
helyzetéből fakad, és nem
személyes vonzerejének
tudható be. A kivetített
szerelem egyetlen, az adott
helyzetből származó, újabb
vonást sem tartalmaz,
kizárólag korábbi, gyermekkori
reakciók ismétléséből áll. Így
az analitikusnak semmi oka,
hogy „hódítására" – ahogyan
az esetet analízisen kívül
nevezhetnénk – büszke legyen,
és mindig jó ha erre
emlékezünk.*

*The analyst must first
recognize that the patient's
falling in love is induced by
the analytic situation and is
not to be attributed to the*

Házasságom Elmával
eldöntöttnek tűnik. Frau G.
nagyon szenved. Csak az
atyai áldás hiányzik.

Marriage with Elma seems
to be decided. Frau G. is
suffering greatly. What is still
missing is the fatherly
blessing.

*charms of his own person.
Transference-love exhibits not
a single new feature arising
from the present situation. It
is entirely composed of repeti-
tions of earlier reactions,
including infantile ones. The
analyst therefore has no
grounds whatever for being
proud of such a 'conquest', as
it would be called outside
analysis, and it is always well
to be reminded of this.*

*Minden bizonnyal óriási sik-
erélményt szerezne a betegnek,
ha szerelme viszonzásra
találna, ez azonban a kezelés
teljes kudarcát is jelentené
egyben. Sikerülne felszínre
hoznia, a valós életben megis-
mételni azt, amire csak
emlékeznie lett volna szabad.
Hasonlóan értelmetlen lenne
kivetített nemiségének elny-
omására ösztönözni a beteget.
Ez annyit jelentene, mintha
egy alvilági szellemet sikeresen
megigézve visszaküldenénk azt,
anélkül hogy akár egyetlen
kérdést is feltettünk volna.
Felszínre hoznánk a tudatalat-
tiba rekesztettet, csakhogy
ijedtünkben újra elnomhassuk.*

*If the patient's love were to be
returned it would be a great
triumph for her, but a complete
defeat for the treatment. She
would have succeeded in acting
out, in repeating in real life,
what she ought only to have
remembered. It would be
equally senseless to urge the
patient to suppress her erotic
transference. It would be just
as if, having summoned a
spirit from the underworld, one
were to send it down again
without having asked it a
single question. One would
have brought the repressed
into consciousness, only to
repress it once more in fright.*

Az utolsó percben, Elma apja
néhány bizonytalan ellen-
vetést tett, és kérte halasszuk
el az eljegyzést. Ezt követően,
meglepetésemre, Elmaban is
kétségek támadtak. Lehullott
szememről a hályog, amikor
nem a szerelmes tiszta
örömét, hanem az érzelmi
sebek fájdalmát vettem észre
rajta. Rá kellett döbbenjek,
nem házasságra, hanem egy
betegség kezelésére kell
törekedjek. Nem tudom
megkímélni önt a fáradságtól,
megkérem vegye kezelés alá
Elmát. Nincsen más lehetőség.
Velem akarja folytatni a
kezelést, de ez természetesen
kizárt.

At the last minute, Elma's
father made a few hesitant
objections and requested her
to postpone the engagement.
Whereupon, to my amazement,
doubts crept into Elma's mind.
The scales fell from my eyes
when, at this moment, she
showed not the pure joy of a
lover but rather the pain of
her emotional wounds. I had
to recognize that the issue
should be one not of marriage
but of the treatment of an
illness. I cannot spare you the
effort and trouble of taking
Elma into treatment. There is
no other way out. She wishes
to continue in treatment with
me – that is naturally out of
the question.

Az analitikus által követendő úthoz nincsen a valós életből átvehető modell. A beteg szerelmét sem viszonozni, sem elnyomni nem szabad. Az analitikusnak vigyáznia kell, nehogy betege eltérjen kivetített érzelmétől, de ugyanilyen határozottan tartózkodnia kell annak viszonzásától. A szerelmet, mint valami valótlan dolgot kell kezelnie, mint egy helyzetet, amin a kezelés során dolgozni kell, amit vissza kell követni tudatalatti forrásáig. A kivetített szerelem eszköz, aminek segítségével a tudat szintjére hozható, tehát ellenőrzés alá vonható mindaz, ami a legmélyebben van elrejtve a beteg nemi életében.

Nincs nagy véleménnyel Elma irántam érzett szerelméről. Ezt persze előre tudtam – de láthatóan nem hittem el teljesen, másként közlései nem csüggesztenének ennyire. Elma esete tehát teljesen elrendeződött. Bár vágyok a fiatalságra és szépségre, tisztán látom a veszélyeket amelyek Elma mellett rám várnak. Elmondtam neki, hogy a doktor és beteg közötti szerelem rendszerint az analízis áldozatául esik, így a házasságra való kilátások minimálisak. Holdkóroshoz hasonló biztonsággal állítottam ezt, figyelmen kívül hagyva a feltörő fájdalmat. Elma reményvesztett volt. Hazakísértem és anyja gondjaiban hagytam. Azóta nem láttam újra.

patient's love must be neither gratified nor suppressed. The analyst must take care not to steer away from the transference-love, but he must just as resolutely withhold any response to it. He must treat the love as something unreal, as a situation which has to be worked through in the treatment and traced back to its unconscious origins. The transference-love must assist in bringing all that is most deeply hidden in the patient's erotic life into her consciousness and therefore under her control.

don't seem to have believed it entirely, otherwise your communication wouldn't have depressed me. So now the case of Elma has been completely settled. Even though I long for youth and beauty I see clearly what dangers I have to look forward to with her. I told her that the affective relations between doctor and patient usually fall victim to the analysis, so that the prospects for a marital union between us were always minimal. I did this with somnabulistic certainty, paying no heed to the painful uproar inside me. Elma was in

despair. I accompanied her home and handed her over to her mother. Since then I haven't seen her.

Mindenek előtt hangsúlyozni kell a beteg ellenállásának téveszthetetlen jelét ebben a valótlan „szerelemben". Egyetértünk abban, hogy a valódi szerelem fokozná a beteg készségét problémáinak megoldására, ha más okból nem, akkor azért mert az általa szeretett személy ezt kéri tőle. Ehelyett azonban azt látjuk, hogy a beteg elvesztette minden érdeklődését a kezelés iránt és világos, hogy nem tiszteli orvosa meggyőződéseit. A szerelem álarca valójában a beteg kezelés iránti ellenállásának megnyilvánulása.

Above all it is necessary to stress to the patient the unmistakable element of

Egészen őszintének éreztem magam, amikor azt mondtam, örülök hogy Elma esete nélkülem is rendeződött. Mégis rendkívül elszomorította, amikor megtudtam, hogy tényleg megtartja esküvőjét az Amerikaival. Tudomásul kellett vennem azt a néhány szálat, amellyel tudatalattim még mindig belékapaszkodik, és hogy ezek a szálak talán erősebbek, mint azt hajlandó voltam beismerni.

I was quite honest when I told you that I am happy to see the matter with Elma

resistance in this unreal 'love'. Genuine love, we say, would intensify her readiness to solve the problems of her case, if for no other reason than that the person she is in love with asks it of her. Instead of this, we point out, she has thrown up all interest in her treatment and clearly feels no respect for her doctor's convictions. In the guise of being in love with him therefore she is really bringing out a resistance to treatment.

settled without me, and yet I was extraordinarily saddened when I learned that her marriage with that American is really going to take place. On this occasion I had to acknowledge that my unconscious is still hanging on to her by a few threads, and that these threads are perhaps stronger than I have been willing to acknowledge.

A kivetített szerelemből nagymértékben hiányzik a valóság érzékelése. Sokkal kevésbé törődik a következményekkel és még inkább vak a szeretett személy értékelésében, mint azt a normális szerelem esetében készek lennénk elismerni. Ebben a kérdésben azonban ténylegesen a mérték a fontos – hiszen ne feledjük, hogy a kivetített szerelem ezen jellemzői pontosan azok, ami minden szerelem lényege.

Transference-love is lacking to a high degree in a regard for reality. It is less concerned about consequences and more blind in its valuation of the loved person than we are prepared to admit in the case of normal love. However, it is a matter of degree – we should not forget that such characteristics of transference-love are precisely what is essential about any state of being in love.

Gizella azzal tölti ki tudatalatti bosszúját, hogy őszinte házassági kérésemre azt az értelmetlen választ adja, hogy előbb Elma jövőjéről kell gondoskodnia. Azt mondja, Elma talán el akar hagyni Amerikai férjét és visszajönni Európába. Azt mondja, meg kell várnia Elma visszatértét. Meg kell jegyeznem, hogy sokkal hűvösebb szexuális közösülés közben, mint korábban volt. Csak akkor lehetek nyugodt házasságunkkal kapcsolatos elhatározása felől, ha ez a tünet megszűnik.

Gizella is taking her unconscious revenge on me by answering my honestly intended offer of marriage with the senseless consideration that she must first be assured of Elma's future. She says Elma perhaps wants to get away from her husband in America and come back to Europe. She says she must await Elma's return. She also cites the possibility that, upon Elma's return, I would again fall in love with Elma. I must note that she has become much cooler in sexual intercourse than she had been earlier. Only when this symptom disappears can I be at peace about her unambiguous will to marry me.

A kivetített szerelem régi vonások újabb kiadásaiból és a gyermekkori reakciók megismétléséből áll. De ez minden szerelem alapvető jellemzője. Nincs olyan állapot, amely ne reprodukálna gyermekkori prototípusokat. A szerelem éppen ettől a gyermeki megrögzöttségtől kapja megszállottságra emlékeztető jellegét, amely már-már a betegesség felé hajlik.

Transference-love consists of new editions of old traits, and repeats infantile reactions. But this is the essential character of every state of being in love. There is no such state

Frau G. férje hozzájárult a váláshoz. Gépiesen végzem a feladatokat, amelyeket Frau G. iránti megváltozott helyzetem megkövetel. De ritka, kettesben töltött pillanataink alatt, kényelmetlenül tudatossá vált bennem e szerelem elvégzésének kötelességszerű jellege. Előrehaladásnak tekintem, hogy nem szóltam erről Frau G.-nek, mint azt korábban az „őszinteség" leple alatt tettem volna.

Frau G.'s husband has agreed to the divorce. I have mechanically taken care of the tasks which my new position with regard to Frau G. required of me. But in our infrequent

which does not reproduce infantile prototypes. It is precisely from this infantile determination that the state of being in love receives its compulsive character, verging as it does on the pathological.

intimate encounters I have become unpleasantly aware of the duty-like character of the execution of this love. A progressive step, in contrast to before, is that I have not told this to Frau G. – as I would have done in the past, under the guise of 'honesty'.

*Az orvos számára nem mindig
könnyű a szakma és az erkölcs
által meghatározott kereteken
belül maradnia. Főként a fiatal-
abbak számára jelenthet ez
nehéz feladatot. A szexuális
szerelem kétségkívül az élet leg-
fontosabb dolgai közé számit, és
a szerelem élvezetében egyesülő
szellemi és testi kielégülés ennek
egyik csúcspontja. Amikor egy nő
szerelmet vár nehéz, lehangoló
feladat egy férfi számára elu-
tasítani közeledését – mert
páratlanul vonzó egy erkölcsös
asszony, amint szerelmét meg-
vallja.*

*It is not always easy for the
doctor to keep within the limits
prescribed by ethics and
technique. Those who are still
youngish may in particular find
it a hard task. Sexual love is
undoubtedly one of the chief
things in life, and the union of
mental and bodily satisfaction
in the enjoyment of love is one
of its culminating peaks. When a
woman sues for love, to reject
and refuse is a distressing part
for a man to play – for there is*

Lichtung

1998–9

A work for the *Weimar 99* festival. Weimar figures prominently in German cultural and political history. It has been home to the Cranachs, to Goethe, Schiller and Nietzsche, to Bach and Liszt. After the First World War the city became the seat of government of the Democratic Republic. During this period the Bauhaus school of design was founded there. Its faculty included Gropius, Mies van der Rohe, Breuer and Moholy-Nagy. In 1933 the Nazis closed the Bauhaus.[1] In 1937 they opened the Buchenwald concentration camp in the Ettersberg forest that borders Weimar. It was in this forest, at Schloss Ettersberg, that Goethe presided over the 'Court of the Muses' that first established Weimar's reputation as a cultural capital. Goethe became a ducal administrator for the Duchy of Saxe-Weimar in 1775 and his association with Weimar continued until his death there in 1832. In Goethe's day a 'hunting star' was maintained in the forest. Animals would be flushed out and driven down paths cut through the woods in the form of a star. Members of the leisure class would lie in ambush where the paths intersected. By the time the 'National Socialists' arrived at the forest the castle had fallen into disrepair. The hunting star had become overgrown, except in places at the edge of the forest where local people came to cut wood. Without the builders of Buchenwald being aware of its history, one of these paths came to provide the principal axis of the concentration camp.

When renovation of Schloss Ettersberg began in preparation for the *Weimar 99* festival, the architect commissioned to undertake the work[2] inaugurated a simple and effective act of rememberance. He ordered the clearing of the long-concealed hunting path that connects the site of Goethe's Court of the Muses to the site of the Buchenwald concentration camp. Visitors to Weimar are now able to walk from one place to the other. The walk is physically arduous. No less difficult is the task of covering the emotional and intellectual ground between the two sites. I was invited by the architect to make a video to be installed in a room in Schloss Ettersberg, which would provide visitors with an occasion for reflection on the walk. As part of my research for the work I read a number of books by Goethe, including his novel of 1809, *Elective Affinities (Die Wahlverwandtschaften)*. The book is an account of the effects on a hitherto stable relationship between a married couple of the landowning class, Edward and Charlotte, when two others are introduced into their household. Edward prevails upon his wife to allow an

1 The Bauhaus was based in Weimar from 1919–25, and in Dessau from 1925–33.

2 Walther Grunwald, Berlin-Weimar.

old friend of his, the Captain, to live with them, and Charlotte responds by bringing her young niece, Ottilie, to live at the house. One commentator has described the book as 'a study in the geometry of changing relationships . . . the topography of shifting attractions and separations among four people.'[3] The book is also an account of the disasters that ensue from the will to plan and control totally. One of the reasons Edward gives for introducing the Captain into the household is that his friend is a skilled surveyor and engineer, and therefore able to help the couple with improvements to their estate. The first task the Captain undertakes is to draw an accurate map of the lands owned by his hosts. This map is used for the first time when the four get together, following a walk around the grounds, to plan the building of a pavilion away from the house:

3 Tony Tanner, *Adultery in the Novel: Contract and Transgression,* Baltimore and London, Johns Hopkins, 1979, p. 179.

. . . at home that evening they straightaway took out the new map . . . 'I would build the pavilion here,' said Ottilie, laying her finger on the highest level place on the hill. 'You could not see the mansion, I know, for it is concealed by the little wood; but . . . you would find yourself in a new and different world . . .'[4]

4 Johann Wolfgang von Goethe, *Elective Affinities,* London, Penguin, 1971, p. 76.

It is this passage, in the original German, that is heard as voice-over on the sound-track of my video. The passage, with its attribution, was stencilled, in several languages, on the wall of the light-trap outside the room where the projection took place. When I first visited Schloss Ettersberg and the park around it I was struck by an uncanny sense of familiarity. I then realized that I was inhabiting the topography that Goethe describes in *Elective Affinities*. Goethe's characters planned a Utopian construction on the hill above Schloss Ettersbeßrg. What would be built in reality over a century later would be the 'new and different world' of Buchenwald.

Single-screen video projection, 1998–9
DVD – 10-minute programme loop – colour – NTSC – stereo

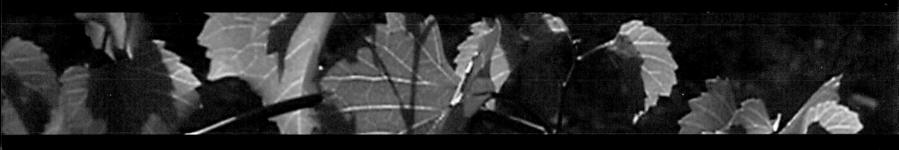

Wolfgang Amadeus Mozart
Die Zauberflöte
Overture [opening bars]

Um sich alles mehr im Einzelnen zu vergegenwärtigen nahm man Abends zu
Hause sogleich die neue Karte vor.
. . . 'Ich würde', sagte Ottilie, indem sie den Finger auf die höchste Fläche
der Anhöhe setzte, 'das Haus hierher bauen. Man sähe zwar das Schloß nicht:
denn es wird von dem Wäldchen bedeckt; aber man befände sich auch dafür
wie in einer andern und neuen Welt.'

. . . einer andern und neuen Welt.

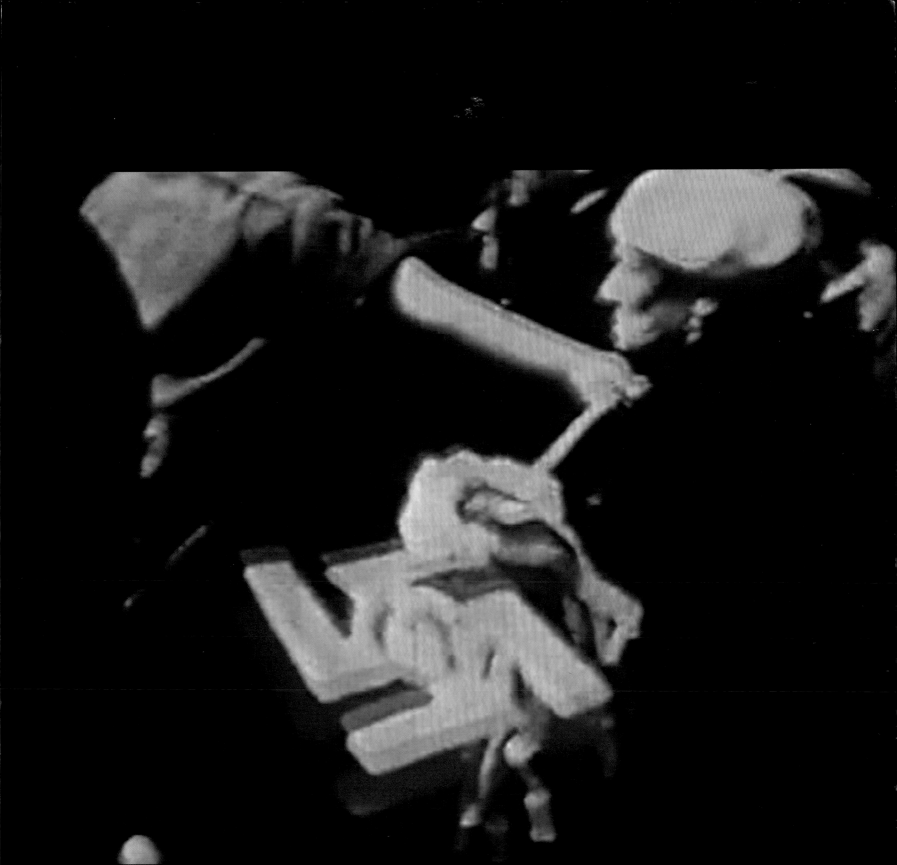

Another Case History

1999

Another Case History is one of a number of works I have made based on Alfred Hitchcock's film *Vertigo*.[1] Hitchcock's film is an adaptation of the novel *D'Entre les Morts,* by Pierre Boileau and Thomas Narcejac, which in turn is derived from the myth of Orpheus and Eurydice. I am not concerned to represent in their entirety the tales told in film, novel and myth. Rather I am interested in the subordinate narratives that comprise them, stories told in fragmentary, laconic and repetitive forms similar to those of daydreams.[2] The image-track of *Another Case History* is suggested by Madeleine's identification with Carlotta and the detective's pursuit of Madeleine. It includes images made at locations seen in *Vertigo:* the Palace of the Legion of Honor, San Francisco, and Big Basin Redwoods. The intertitles refer to the scene of the rescue from the water. The component narrative may be summarized as follows:

Madeleine is haunted by her forebear Carlotta. Carlotta drowned herself after her lover abandoned her. Madeleine is now the same age Carlotta was when she died and is obsessed by thoughts of her own death. Arranging her hair in the style worn by Carlotta she wanders through the city. The detective follows her. Madeleine throws herself into the water and is rescued by the detective.

Two fragments from the 'event list' are represented as scenes with duration but no development: 'Madeleine is looking at Carlotta', 'the detective is looking at Madeleine'. Another item, the rescue from the water, is represented twice over but with different intertitle sequences. If this work were an opera it might be called a *pasticcio,* as it is assembled from elements I have used in other works. Most of the image-track of *Another Case History* is composed of edited material from *Case History,* a two-screen work shot in San Francisco and Paris. The intertitles on the screen are both used in previous works in which I make reference to *Vertigo.* The first title sequence is from the 30-minute video *Venise,* 1993,[3] shot in San Francisco and Marseille, and is an edited extract from *D'Entre les Morts,* which is set in these two cities. The other title sequence is from a 1984 photo-text work, *The Bridge,* which steers closer to the classical myth.[4] The music on the sound-track of *Another Case History* is from the accompanied recitative of Eurydice's farewell in Act Two of Haydn's opera, *Orfeo ed Euridice.*[5]

---

1 The series begins with the photographic installation *The Bridge* (1984). It continues with *Venise* (1993, 30 minute video), *Study for Case History* (1998, two-monitor video installation) and *Case History* (1998, two-screen video projection). *Another Case History* was first shown in the context of the exhibition *Foul Play* at Thread Waxing Space, New York, in October 1999.

2 Such an initiative may be framed not only by psychoanalytic theory but by work in the structural analysis of narrative. See, for example, Roland Barthes's essay 'The Sequence of Actions' (1973), in *The Semiotic Challenge,* New York, Hill and Wang, 1988.

3 Published in book form as *Venise,* London, Black Dog Publishing, 1997.

4 This work is reproduced in *Between,* London, 1986, and *Passages,* Villeneuve d'Ascq, 1991.

5 Haydn's *Orfeo ed Euridice* was completed in 1790 but not performed until 1950. The libretto is by Carlo Francesco Badini. The fragment heard on the sound-track of the video is sung by Cecilia Bartoli on L'Oiseau Lyre CD 452 668-2.

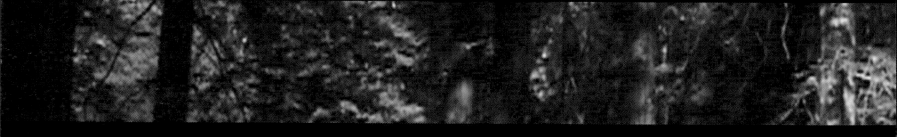

Franz Joseph Haydn
Orfeo ed Euridice
Act II
Accompanied recitative (fragment), Cecilia Bartoli

Her eyelids trembled open   He took her hand   'You're not dead,' he said   He pressed her fingers to his lips

'Never look back,' he said

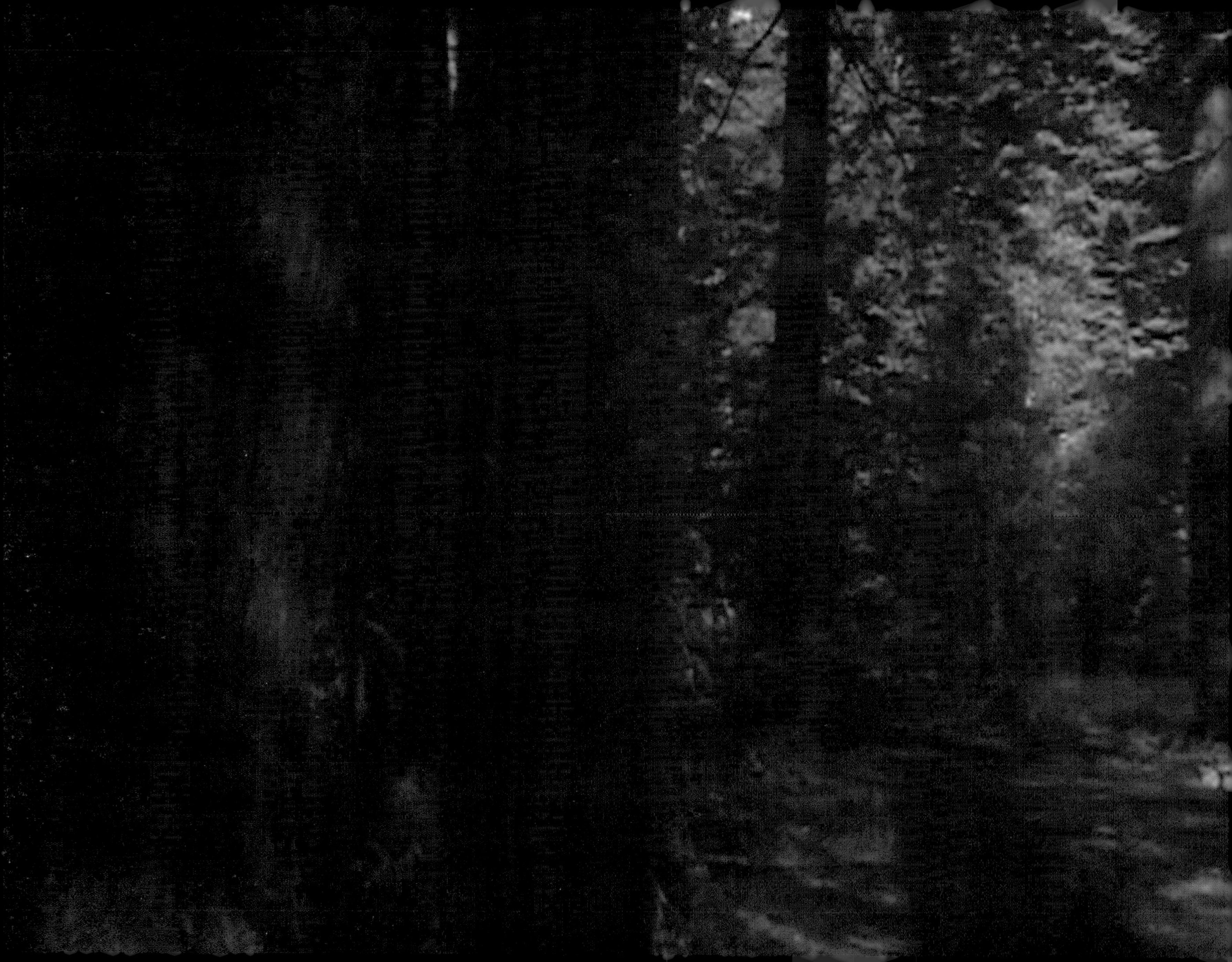

Silently   Violently   The waters break   Around the emerging form

Of a woman   Her tanned flanks   Streaming water   She folds a towel

Around her new-born body   Long shadows of palms   Lie   Across the pool

Falling   Upon the glass walls   Of the corridor   Where he takes his last case

From the room   And closes the door

Nietzsche's Paris

1999–2000

The year 2000 is the centenary of the death, in Weimar, of Friedrich Nietzsche. Three years after his death Elisabeth Förster-Nietzsche, his sister, established the Nietzsche Archive in the house in which he died. She commissioning the Belgian architect Henry van de Velde to reconstruct the entrance and ground-floor reception rooms, and the archive is now as much a place of pilgrimage for admirers of van de Velde's Art Nouveau design as it is for students of Nietzsche's philosophy. After I had completed work on my video for Schloss Ettersberg it was suggested – by architects with a particular interest in van de Velde's design – that I might be interested in producing a work in relation to the Nietzsche centenary.

After Nietzsche's death his sister worked tirelessly to ensure that his work was appropriated by the Fascists. This can only be done by heavily editing Nietzsche. He despised nationalism. He said he was a bad German, but a very good European. He was contemptuous of German culture to the point of denying that there was such a thing. He said on numerous occasions that Europe would be nowhere without the Jews, and spoke out vehemently against the anti-semitism that his sister embraced. Nevertheless, Förster-Nietzsche's version of Nietzsche has prevailed. In the post-war years the communist administration of Weimar placed a pall of disapprobation over Nietzsche that has not yet fully lifted. The architects' proposal led to no specific project in Weimar, but it did lead me to reopen the long-neglected Nietzsche volumes on my shelves, and start to read about his life. During the summer when I was doing this reading I was asked to propose a video work for the Architectural Association in London. I was living in Paris at the time, so I was suddenly presented with a very particular conjunction of terms: Nietzsche, architecture, Paris. The resulting video is an attempt to bring these disparate terms together in a single space.

Nietzsche never visited Paris. The more I read during that summer the stranger this seemed. He was familiar with many European cities. He was especially enthusiastic in his admiration for French culture. French was the only language he knew well apart from his own. The city must have occupied a privileged place in his imagination. The reason why Nietzsche never visited Paris is suggested in his correspondence with Paul Rée and Lou Salomé. In April 1882, while in Rome, Nietzsche met, and apparently fell in love with, Salomé. During that same spring Nietzsche, Salomé and their mutual friend

Paul Rée made plans to set up an intellectual *ménage à trois*. The idea of living together came from Salomé and originally concerned only herself and Rée. But the two readily agreed that Nietzsche be included. Nietzsche suggested they should live in Paris, He set about contacting friends who might find a suitable apartment. The three were still discussing their Paris plans when they met again, in Leipzig, in November. Then quite abruptly Salomé and Rée left the city, without warning anyone, or leaving any indication of where they had gone. The abandoned Nietszche assumed, incorrectly, that they were in Paris.

Though it ended in bitter estrangement, the short-lived relationship between Nietzsche and Salomé had passed through an idyllic space of intimacy during the three weeks in August they spent together debating philosophy in the forest of Tautenberg. The historical association between forests, gardens and learning is exploited by Dominique Perrault in the recently completed Bibliothèque Nationale de France. Perrault's sunken forest garden at the centre of the site has been appropriately described by one commentator as 'an untouchable Eden from which researchers and members of the public are barred.'[1] In memory of Nietzsche's edenic period with the unattainable Lou it is this Paris site that appears in the work.

Lou Salomé said that the idea of living together with Rée had come to her in a dream. She writes:

I saw a pleasant study filled with books and flowers, between two bedrooms, and, coming and going amongst us, comrades in thought forming an intellectual circle at once serious and gay.[2]

This sentence is spoken on the sound-track in the original German. Part of it appears in translation as a title sequence.

150

1 Barbara-Ann Campbell,
Paris: A guide to recent architecture,
London, Ellipsis/Könemann, 1997, p. 172.

2 Lou Andreas-Salomé, *Looking Back,*
New York, Marlow & Company, 1995, p. 45.

George Frederich Handel
Alcina
Act II Scene VIII

Da erblickte ich nämlich eine angenehme Arbeitsstube voller Bücher und
Blumen, flankiert von zwei Schlafstuben und – bei uns hin und her gehend –
Arbeitskameraden, zu heiterem und ernstem Kreis geschlossen.

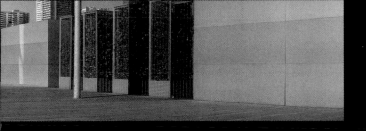

I saw   a pleasant workroom

George Frederick Handel
Ariodante
Act II Scene III
Aria: 'Scherza Infida In Grembo Al Drudo' (fragment), Anne Sofie von Otter

filled   with   books and flowers   between

two   bedrooms

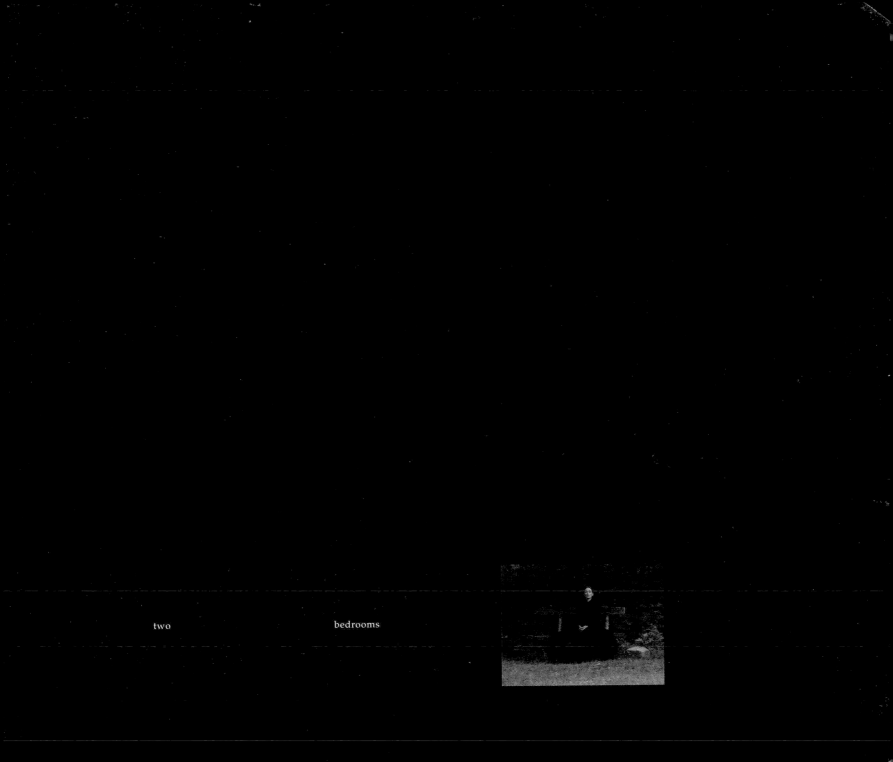

Elective Affinities

2000

Often, an essay or a video begins with a presentiment, something that cannot be known in advance of research and writing, shooting and editing. I am in Barcelona to work on a retrospective exhibition for the Fundació Antoni Tàpies. I find the genius of the place, which for me is where my internal world and the social and historical reality of the city intersect, in Mies van der Rohe's pavilion for the 1929 International Exhibition. Embarrassing, as if I had gone to Paris and discovered the Eiffel tower. I must nevertheless accept the fact that the pavilion haunts me. It remains to be seen why.

Before I visited Barcelona, I had admired the Mies building as one milestone in modernism amongst others. I know therefore that if the pavilion haunts me now it is because Barcelona haunts the pavilion. I climb from the Plaça d'Espanya to the site of the 1929 building and its 1986 reincarnation. I enter the pavilion only to find myself leaving. The space behaves like a moebius strip. I feel I am in one of those folds in space-time dear to science-fiction writers. I recall one such story: a rollercoaster at an amusement park has unwittingly been constructed with such a geometry that those who first take the ride emerge decades from the point at which they began. I feel I might emerge from the reconstructed pavilion into the Barcelona of 1929, with history poised almost motionless before the vertiginous descent that leads to the Fascist occupation of the city a decade later. I take another turn through the building. No point of rest in this elusive space, but a point of reference: Georg Kolbe's statue of a standing figure. The bronze, titled *Dawn*, shows a woman raising her arms to shade her face from the light. The title disavows the violence implicit in this image of a woman cornered; arms raised and face averted, as if turning from an undisclosed horror.

On the slopes of Montjuic, I find myself thinking again of the pavilion on the hill in *Die Wahlverwandtschaften*. Goethe's novella suggests natural affinities between rationalism and disaster, perspective and dismay. The panorama surveyed from the hilltop is calm and intelligible, but conceals as much as it reveals. Eight slender cruciform columns support the roof of the pavilion, chromed to render them all but invisible. The roof also receives support from heavier structures hidden behind stone cladding. Reading about the meticulous assembling of information through which the pavilion was reconstructed[1] I am reminded of a police investigation, as if I am visiting the scene of a crime. What part did Lilly Reich play in this affair? Why did Mies accept Kolbe's bronze, when it was not what he wanted? Back home, I reopen the file. Amongst materials I had put to one side in anticipation of my visit to Barcelona is a tape of a French television programme about Catalonia and the Civil War. Mainly talking heads, with scraps of film footage scattered between. In one fleeting fragment a smiling woman, rifle over her shoulder, raises her arm to shade her face.

1 See, for example, Ignasi de Solà-Morales, Cristian Cirici, Fernando Ramos, *Mies Van Der Rohe Barcelona Pavilion*, Barcelona, Gustavo Gili, 1998.

Elective Affinities

Video projection, work in progress
DVD – colour –NTSC – stereo

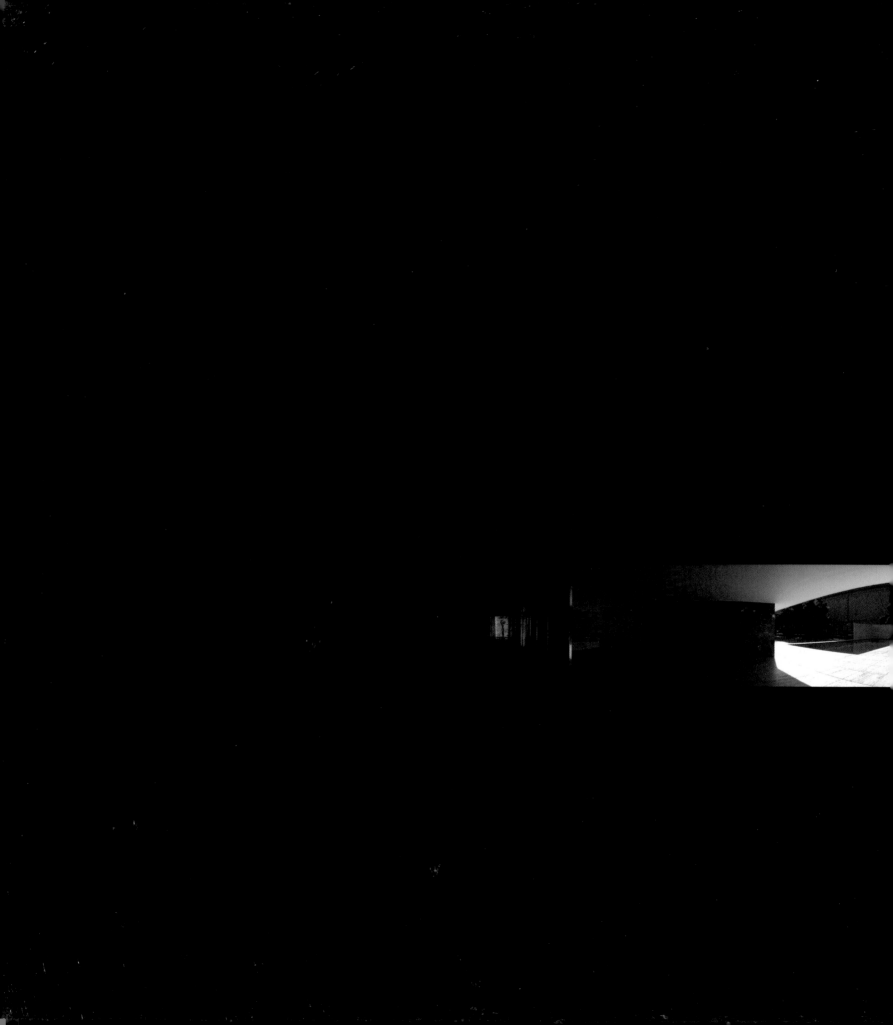

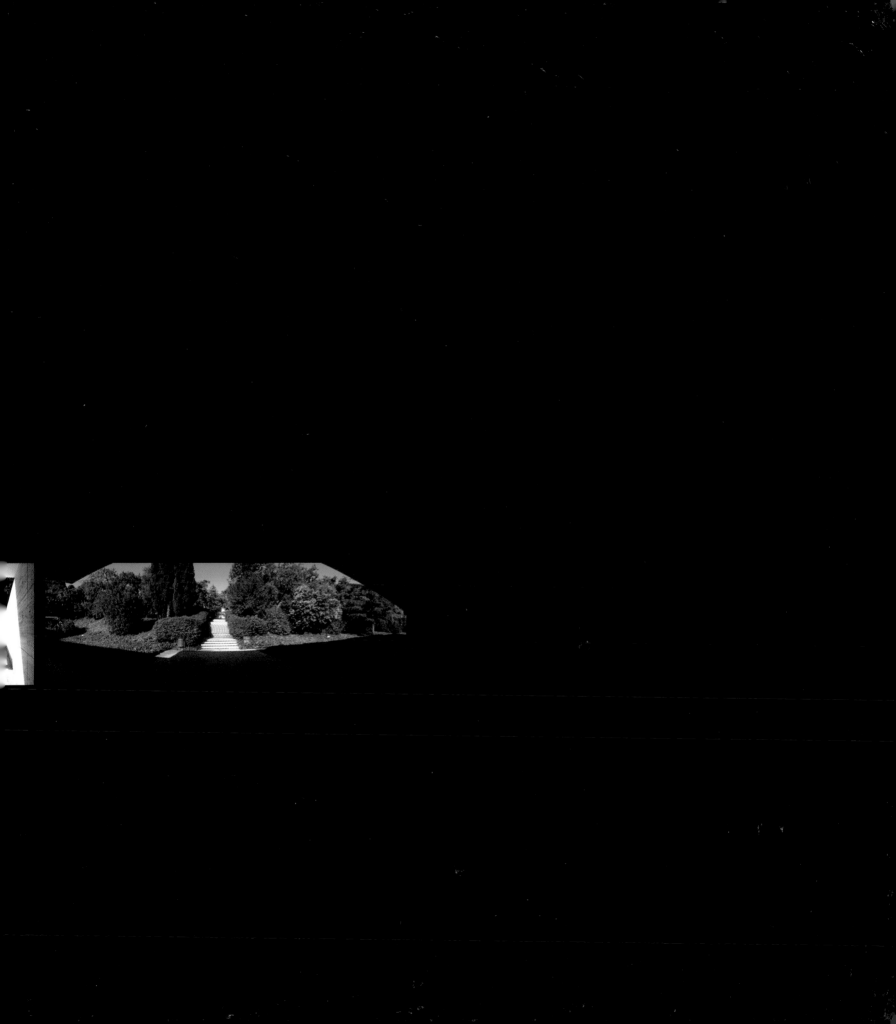

'Thus the shadow of the object fell upon the ego'

Sigmund Freud, *Mourning and Melancholia*